PRESENTED TO:

....

FROM:

....

DATE:

....

INDESCRIBABLE

100 DEVOTIONS ABOUT GOD & SCIENCE

LOUIE GIGLIO

WITH TAMA FORTNER

ILLUSTRATED BY
NICOLA ANDERSON

passionpublishing

Tommy Nelson

An Imprint of Thomas Nelson

CONTENTS

INTRODUCTION

When was the last time you said the word *awesome*? Maybe you were talking about one of your favorite sports stars, your favorite snack, or your favorite shoes. I think French fries and sneakers and basketball stars are all pretty awesome, but in this book, I want to tell you about the *most* awesome thing in the world: the great God who created the entire awesome universe and everything that exists in it.

God's Word, the Bible, tells us that the heavens proclaim God's glory and creativity every day and night. The stars don't speak in words like we do, but how big they are and the way they shine so bright tell us that the God who created them is amazing and powerful. That's why it's important and fun for us to spend time exploring and learning about everything our God has made. The more we learn about what He's created, the more we learn about Him.

Sometimes, I like to think about God as a scientist in a lab coat, eager to share with us all the incredible things He's made in His indescribable, immeasurable universe-size lab. You know what? Not only does God love science—He is the greatest scientist of all!

Throughout this book, we'll explore the incredibly, indescribably awesome universe that God created and holds in His hands. I asked some friends to help us along the way. Meet Evyn, Raz, Norah, Joshua, Clarke, and Adelynn. These kids, just like you, are eager to learn about everything God has made.

Each day, we'll read together about a different part of God's creation, from space, to earth, to animals, to people. We'll look at real-life pictures and illustrations, learn scientific facts, and pray to our Creator God together.

If you're interested in focusing on a certain part of the universe for a while, feel free to skip around this book as much as you'd like! The four major topics we'll talk about are:

My prayer is that you'll be truly amazed and in awe as we learn that the God who created Betelgeuse, one of the biggest stars we know about, also created YOU—from the number of hairs on your head to the color of the skin on your toes. This indescribable Creator knows you better and loves you more than anyone on Earth ever could.

Have fun on your journey!

Pastor Louie

1

A BLANK PAGE

In the beginning God created the sky and the earth. The earth was empty and had no form. . . . Then God said, "Let there be light!"

—GENESIS 1:1–3

Every picture and story starts with a blank page. Nothing is on it, and it's yours to do anything with it. That's exactly what happened when God "sat down" to create Earth, the universe, and everything in it. He started with a blank page. Well, actually, there wasn't even a page—just darkness and nothing . . . and God too, of course. Then He started to create, and it was exactly

what He wanted. Planets spun into space, stars stretched across the heavens, and galaxy upon galaxy swirled out into the universe.

All throughout the universe, and here on the Earth, God shows His creativity to be indescribably, incredibly amazing! Who else could think up the spotted, long-necked giraffe? Who else could put the roar in a lion's mouth and the purr in a kitten's tummy? Who else could think up stick bugs, sloths, leafy sea dragons, platypuses, or colorful mantis shrimp? (Seriously, you *need* to check these guys out! They're unbelievable!)

God is infinitely creative—that means His creativity has no end. And God shows His creativity in *you*. You began as a blank page in His book, and He began writing your story before you were even born. It's going to be a great one! Don't believe it? Just check out some of the amazing stories He's already written for "ordinary" people just like you—David knocking out Goliath, Daniel napping with lions, and Esther saving her people. God's got an amazing story in the works for you—just wait and see!

Lord, the whole universe shows Your creativity! I trust that You're creating a wonderful story for me.

BE AMAZED

Sloths are so slow that they move only about 6½ feet per minute. Even their tummies are slow, taking an average of 16 days to digest the twigs, fruits, leaves, bugs, lizards, and birds they eat. They spend almost their entire lives hanging upside down in the trees—coming down only once a week or so to poop. *Ick!*

2

THE SOUNDS OF SILENCE

Lord, every morning you hear my voice. Every morning, I tell you what I need. And I wait for your answer.
—PSALM 5:3

Did you know that you could be right next to someone in space, shouting at the top of your lungs, and that person wouldn't hear a thing? That's not because those space helmets get in the way. It's because voices travel as *sound waves,* and sound waves need something to travel on—like the atmosphere on Earth. Since there's no atmosphere in space, sound waves have nothing to travel on. So astronauts have to talk to each other using a different kind of wave: *radio waves*, which don't need atmosphere to carry them.

But God doesn't need sound waves or even radio waves to hear us. That's because prayers carry our voices to God. So if the God who created the entire universe is ready to listen to whatever we have to say, why don't we pray more?

At least part of the answer is that we get distracted and busy. The busyness of school, church, sports, family, friends, and a zillion other things gets in the way. Then there's texting and video games and TV shows and movies and computer work. On average, we spend almost eight hours a day staring at some sort of screen, like a TV, computer, or phone. That's almost sixty hours every week!

In the middle of all of these fun, cool, and exciting things, God calls us to "be still" (Psalm 46:10) and pray to Him. Praying is when we praise God for who He is, thank Him for all He's given us, and ask Him for what we need.

Try it today. Find a special place where you can be alone with God. In a treehouse, in a corner of your room, or even in a bubble bath. Be still, talk to God, and listen for Him to answer. And, remember, God usually speaks with a still, small voice—so be sure to listen closely.

God, thank You for wanting to spend time with me. Thank You for always listening to me and answering my prayers.

BE AMAZED

Praying is so important that Jesus—God's own Son—took time to pray. Check out some of the ways Jesus prayed in Luke 5:16, Luke 6:12, and Matthew 14:23.

3

DINOSAURS AND DRAGONS—OH MY!

Be strong in the Lord and in his great power. Wear the full armor of God.
—EPHESIANS 6:10–11

Did you know dragons and dinosaurs are in the Bible? Check this out from Job 41:

> "Can you catch Leviathan on a fishhook? . . . If you put one hand on him, you will never forget the battle. . . . He has rows of shields on his back. . . . Flames blaze from his mouth. . . . The sword that hits him does not hurt him. The darts and spears, small and large, do not hurt him. He treats iron as if it were straw. . . . He is a creature without fear." (vv. 1, 8, 15, 19, 26–27, 33)

Some people try to say the Leviathan is just a crocodile. But that doesn't sound like any crocodile I've ever seen! Rather, the word *dragon* comes to mind. And then there's this in Job 40:

> "Look at Behemoth. . . . Look at the strength he has in his body. The muscles of his stomach are powerful! His tail extends like a cedar tree. The muscles of his thighs are woven together. His bones are like tubes of bronze metal. His legs are like bars of iron." (vv. 15, 18)

Again, some people say the Behemoth is an elephant. But have you ever seen an elephant with a tail like a cedar tree?

God made some amazingly strong things. But the strongest is something He actually makes just for you. It's called the armor of God, and it's stronger

than even Leviathan's "rows of shields" (Job 41:15). This armor has a piece to cover every part of you—including your heart and mind—with the power of God and His truth. It will protect you from the devil and all his lies. (Read more about the armor in Ephesians 6:10–18.) So like a knight dressing for battle, put on your armor every day. How? By praying and reading the truth of His Word!

Thank You, God, for Your armor. Teach me how to put it on and wear it every day.

BE AMAZED

The acid in your stomach is so powerful it can melt metal. But an armor of mucus protects your stomach lining and keeps that acid in your tummy, where it belongs, so the acid breaks down only what it's supposed to!

4

WHAT'S THAT SMELL?!?

"Woe to you . . . you hypocrites! You are like whitewashed tombs, which look beautiful on the outside but on the inside are full of the bones of the dead and everything unclean."

—MATTHEW 23:27 NIV

Doesn't that flower smell . . . *horrible?* While most flowers smell wonderful, if you got a whiff of this monster—the titan arum—you'd run. Why? Well,

consider its nickname, the "corpse flower," and that just might give you a clue. In case you didn't know—a *corpse* is a rotting, dead body. *Yuck!*

The corpse flower grows in Indonesia and is one of the world's largest and rarest flowers. Its stalk can grow up to 15 feet tall, and its bloom can be more than 3 feet wide—that's the length of a yardstick! But even with its amazing size, the corpse flower is best known for its foul odor. Its bloom smells rotten. *Ugh!* In fact, it even looks rotten. But all of this grossness makes it positively irresistible to insects, which the plant needs for pollination, so it can reproduce and make *more* big, stinky flowers.

The outside of the corpse flower is actually kind of pretty, even though it smells like rotting flesh. Basically, it's the hypocrite of the plant world. What's a *hypocrite*, you ask? That's a big, fancy word for someone who pretends to be good only when people are watching. But when no one's watching, they do the wrong things. You could also call them *two-faced* or *phony*. Their insides and outsides don't match. Have you ever met anyone like that? Well, Jesus said that's no way to live. Your words and actions should always be good and loving—whether anyone is watching or not. Now *that's* a life that will smell sweet.

BE AMAZED

The Venus flytrap is one of the world's deadliest plants—if you're a bug, that is. Its leaves are actually a hinged trap. When a bug crawls in, it "tickles" the hairlike fibers on the leaves. This triggers the trap, and the leaves snap shut, trapping the insect inside—where it is slowly digested!

Dear God, I don't want my life to be stinky or phony or two-faced. Fill my heart with Your love, and help me do the right thing even when no one is watching.

5

HOW DEEP IS THE DEEP?

Lord, you have examined me. You know all about me. You know when I sit down and when I get up. You know my thoughts before I think them.

—PSALM 139:1–2

The oceans are beautiful, amazing, and mysterious places—at least to us. God, of course, knows all about them! Even though oceans cover more than 70 percent of the Earth's surface, we have only explored about 5 percent of them. That's at least partly because of how deep they are. The average depth of the ocean is 12,100 feet—that's more than 2 miles deep!

Parts of the ocean are so deep that scientists have not yet been able to explore them. But what they have explored has led to some amazing discoveries—like the giant sunfish, which can weigh up to 5,000 pounds; the fangtooth fish, whose nightmarish fangs make it look like something out of a scary movie; and the blobfish, which looks like . . . well . . . a 12-inch blob of pink goo. Scientists believe millions more species are just waiting to be discovered under the sea. And while we may not yet know all the mysteries of the ocean deep, we can trust that God does.

God also knows all the mysteries of the deepest places of your mind. He knows every thought before you even think it—the good ones and the not-so-good ones. God understands there are times when a bad thought will sneak into your head, even though you don't want it to. Don't give up or be discouraged. But don't keep thinking those bad thoughts either—"capture" them, and "make [them] give up and obey Christ" (2 Corinthians 10:5). It can be tough to do, but ask God for His help—you know He'll help you do it!

BE AMAZED

The deepest part of the ocean (that we know of) is located inside the Mariana Trench in the Pacific Ocean. It's called the Challenger Deep, and it's approximately 36,070 feet deep. If you were to drop Mount Everest, the world's highest mountain, into the Challenger Deep, it would be covered by more than a mile of water!

Lord, You know everything about me—even every thought that I think. Help me capture any bad thoughts that wander in, and fill my mind with thoughts of You instead.

6

HOLDING IT TOGETHER!

[Christ] is before all things, and in him all things hold together.
—COLOSSIANS 1:17 NIV

Have you ever seen workers build a brick building? They don't just stack the bricks on top of each other. They need some sort of glue to hold all those bricks together. The glue for bricks is called *mortar*.

In the same way, your body is made up of 37.2 trillion little bricks called *cells*. And like a building, those cells need some sort of glue to hold them all together. The glue for cells is called *laminin*.

Laminin holds *your body* together. The thing that's even more amazing about laminin is what it looks like. When you take a peek at laminin (and you'll need an electron microscope to see it), it looks like . . . *a cross*.

Why is that important? Because it's yet another reminder that we are God's own creation. You see, God left His fingerprints all throughout His creation. The Bible tells us that even though we can't see the invisible qualities of God—like His awesome power and His holiness—we can see His creation and know He is real (Romans 1:20). Jesus was with God at creation, and "in him all things were created: things in heaven and

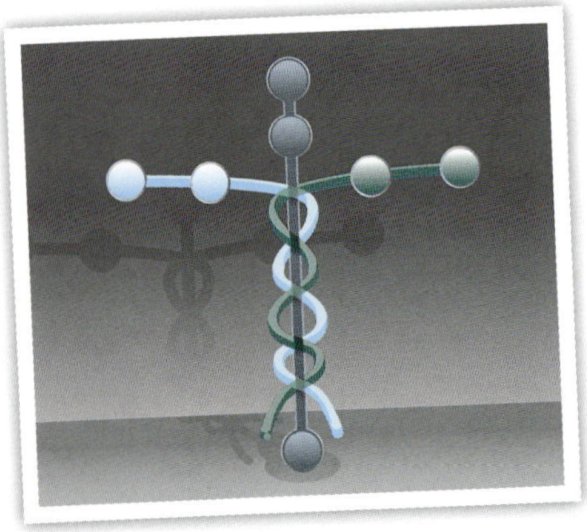
Laminin

BE AMAZED

The earliest known use of glue was birch bark tar, which was used to make spears. The earliest written record of the use of glue comes from ancient Egypt. Hieroglyphs show that the casket of Pharaoh Tutankhamun (you may know him as King Tut) was glued together with a glue made from animal bones and skin.

on earth, visible and invisible. . . . In him all things hold together" (Colossians 1:16–17 NIV).

Laminin is a picture of what Jesus tells us in His Word—He is the glue that holds our bodies, our souls, and everything together. So when you're feeling overwhelmed and having the absolute worst day ever, think about laminin—and remember that Jesus holds you—and all things—together.

Lord, when I start to worry about all the things happening in my life and around me, help me remember You are Lord of all—and You hold everything, including me, together.

7

FASTER THAN THE SPEED OF LIGHT

God said, "Let there be light!"
And there was light.
—GENESIS 1:3

Have you ever wished you'd been there to see God create the world? I mean, how amazing would it have been to see how He did it all?

It would've been breathtaking and overwhelming. Why? Because when God said, "Let there be light!" there wasn't just the flick of a universal light switch. No way! This was more like a light explosion that would have been way more than your eyes could handle.

The Bible tells us in Psalm 33:6 that the heavens were made by the word of God. He *breathed* out the universe and everything in it. So when God said He wanted light—that light came flying out of His mouth at 186,000 miles *per second*! That's how fast light travels, so we call it the "speed of light." God's light streaked across the heavens, chased back the darkness, and lit up the entire universe in a blaze of brilliant glory.

Only one thing is faster than the speed of light, and that's the speed of God. When you call out to God in prayer, He's instantly right there to listen—and He starts working on His answer right away. The thing is, though, God may not give you that answer right away. Sometimes He asks you to wait for it, and sometimes He might not give you the answer you want. But you can trust that God will always give you the exact, right answer—at just the right moment and in just the right way. He's always working faster than the speed of light!

God, I can't even begin to imagine how fast light really is. And to know that You hear my prayers even faster than that is amazing to me. Thank You, God, for rushing to listen to me!

BE AMAZED

God's universe is so big that it can't be measured in feet or inches or even miles. We have to use a bigger ruler: the *light-year*. A light-year is—you guessed it—how far light travels in a year, which is 5.88 trillion miles. Our own Milky Way Galaxy is 100,000 light-years wide. And that's just one galaxy out of the billions that our mighty God created!

8

A TOOL FOR GOD

Encourage one another and build each other up.

—1 THESSALONIANS 5:11 NIV

Scientists have long known that some animals use tools to help them get what they need. But they have only recently discovered the most unusual way one animal "builds" its house—and they found this animal scurrying across the sands of the ocean floor.

The veined octopus (*Amphioctopus marginatus*) builds its home using coconut shell halves that people have thrown into the ocean. Stacking one on top of the other, it crawls between the two halves—the perfect underwater armor for this soft-bodied octopus. When the octopus needs to travel, it simply stacks the shell halves under its body—much like stacking two bowls. It then "stilt walks" on its eight legs, dragging the shells with it. Scientists have even spotted veined octopuses digging buried coconut shells out of the sand and squirting them with jets of water to clean them before moving in.

God gave some animals the ability to use tools, but did you know that He made you to *be* a tool? God wants you to be His tool in building up others and leading them to Him. How can you do that? He tells you in His Word:

> "Go and make followers of all people in the world. Baptize them in the name of the Father and the Son and the Holy Spirit. Teach them to obey everything that I have told you." (Matthew 28:19–20)

What an amazing thought—that God uses you to build His Kingdom and to help others know Him!

Lord, I want to be a tool in building Your kingdom. Help me live a life that tells the world about You.

BE AMAZED

The veined octopus is just one of several animals that uses tools. There's a group of bottlenose dolphins in Shark Bay, Australia, that carries sea sponges in their beaks to stir up the ocean sand and uncover their prey. Also, sea otters use stones as hammers to crack open abalone shells to get to the food inside.

9

NO BONES ABOUT IT

When a believing person prays,
great things happen.
—JAMES 5:16 NCV

Bones—they're what separate us from the jellyfish. Well . . . bones, intelligence, souls, and a few other things. But the point is that bones are *hugely* important. The adult body has 206 bones—and more than half of them are in your hands and feet. The *femur* (thighbone) is the longest, while the *stapes* (which is in your middle ear) is the smallest.

Bones do many things for your body. For example, bones keep you standing tall. They make up your skeleton and give your body its shape. Bones provide a frame for your muscles so you can move, and they protect your soft tissues and organs. They also store minerals your body needs, like calcium. And bone marrow—the stuff inside your bones—is actually a factory for your blood cells. So, yes, the bones of your skeleton are pretty important, but they aren't the *only* bones you have.

You also need to have healthy "bones of faith." You keep these bones healthy by praying to God, praising Him, studying His Word, and being with His people. The bones of faith are some of the most important bones you need to shape your life. They help keep you moving in the right direction as you follow God's will. They protect the soft insides of your heart and soul. And they store up the power of God in your spirit, so it's there when you need it. If you keep your bones of faith healthy, these bones will keep you standing tall when temptations and tough times come. Make no bones about it—these bones of faith are *hugely* important!

Lord, show me how to keep my "bones of faith" strong so I can always stand tall for You!

BE AMAZED

You were actually born with 300 bones in your body, but now you have only 206. What happened? Did you lose some? No, but some of them did grow together. For example, when babies are born, the bones in their skull are still separate. They're connected only by tough membranes called *fontanelles*—these create the "soft spot" on a baby's head. Over time, the bones grow together and become solid.

10

THE STORY OF THE STARS

The heavens tell the glory of God. And the skies announce what his hands have made. Day after day they tell the story. Night after night they tell it again.

—PSALM 19:1–2

Did you ever go to story time at the library? Or listen as your parents or grandparents told you a story? There's something about *listening* to a story that is just . . . well . . . magical. Perhaps it's because you can close your eyes, lie back, and let your imagination soar.

Did you know that God tells stories too? He tells the very best ones, and He uses the stars to do it. And the story those stars tell isn't just a sweet, soft tale about how they twinkle and shine. No, their story is one of majesty and might and power. It's the story of a God who created everything you can see and everything you cannot see. Their story is shouted—*blasted*—across the universe, through the sky, and down to you. They don't use words to tell their story; they use their presence. For nothing so perfect, so majestic, could have just happened by accident. They had to have a Grand Creator—God.

God *makes* the stars! He is awesome. He is incredible. He is indescribable! And this God who makes the stars . . . also made you.

God wants to fill your life with His story. Just look up at the stars and start to listen: *In the beginning, God created the heavens and the earth* . . . (Genesis 1:1 NIV). Like the stars, you are a part of His story. And you were made to tell everyone how amazing the Creator is.

Lord, just thinking that the One who created the stars wants to make me part of His story is amazing! Thank You! Open my ears to hear the story Your creation tells, and then help me tell it too.

BE AMAZED

Stars don't really twinkle at all. It *looks* as if they do because our atmosphere causes the starlight to bend slightly as it makes its way to the Earth. Our atmosphere is made up of gas-filled air that is always moving (think of it like the wind). The light moves through the atmosphere as the atmosphere moves too. That's what makes stars seem to twinkle.

11

YAKETY-YAK

How many are your works, LORD! In wisdom you made them all; the earth is full of your creatures.
—PSALM 104:24 NIV

Imagine swimming in an ice-cold, freezing pond during the dead of winter—high up in the Himalayan Mountains, where even the trees don't grow. Impossible, you say? Not if you're a yak.

Or how would you feel about going for a stroll outside in temperatures as low as 40 degrees below zero? (That's way colder than it takes for snow to fall!) Crazy, right? Not if you're a yak.

Would you like to dig through layers of thick ice with your 3-foot-long horns just to get something to eat? Ridiculous, you say? Not if you are—you guessed it—a yak.

Why am I yakking on and on about yaks? Simply this, God gives all of His creatures everything they need to live. Why does that matter? Because as God's most treasured creation, you can know God will give you everything you need to live the life He created for you. So if you find yourself needing to do something hard, you can trust God to give you everything you need to do it.

Need to apologize to a friend? God can help you be humble. Need to forgive someone? God can help with that too. (After all, He's pretty great at forgiving you!) Need to change your attitude? God can—you guessed it—show you just what you need to do.

Sure, God asks you to do some tough things sometimes, but He never asks you do them alone. So instead of yakking about whatever is troubling you, turn to God. He's ready to help you.

God, thank You for giving me all I need to live the life You want me to live. Help me always to turn to You—when I need help and when I think I don't.

BE AMAZED

Yaks live in the Himalayas, a mountain range in Tibet that has the world's highest mountain. *Himalayas* means "abode of snow" or "house of snow." At the tops of the mountain range—which reach as high as 29,029 feet at Mount Everest—the ice and snow never melt. But at the bottom of the mountains are tropical forests where elephants and tigers live.

12

THE STAR COUNTER

Look up to the skies. Who created all these stars? He leads out all the army of heaven one by one. He calls all the stars by name. He is very strong and full of power. So not one of them is missing.

—ISAIAH 40:26

A *galaxy* is a gigantic collection of stars, dust, and gas all held together by gravity. Earth, the Sun, and all the other planets that make up our solar system are just a tiny part of our galaxy called the Milky Way Galaxy. The Milky Way is so huge that scientists think between 100 billion and 400 billion stars are in it! They don't know exactly how many because there are just too many stars to count. But the Bible tells us that God counts each and every star. *And* He calls them all by name. Oh, and by the way, that's not just the stars in the Milky Way Galaxy. God counts and names each star in all of the billions and billions of galaxies that we know about—and the billions and billions of galaxies that we haven't even discovered yet. That's how big and how great and how awesome our God is.

God is bigger than anything we have ever seen or anything we could ever dream of or imagine. He is huge, and His universe is ginormous! But do you know what's even more astonishing and wonderful? That same God who knows the stars' names also knows *your* name.

Looking up into the sky might make you feel small—like a tiny, little speck floating in the vastness of space—but *you* are important to God. He knows you and loves you and wants to be the most important part of your life. He wants to build a relationship with you that will never, ever, ever end.

God, I look up at all those stars, and I am amazed that You know all their names. Most of all, I'm so glad that You know my name.

BE AMAZED

If you wanted to try to count all the stars we know about in the Milky Way Galaxy, how long would it take you? By counting one star each second, it would take you 3,168 years! Next time you're outside at night, see how many stars you can count. But don't stay out there for thousands of years!

13

EVEN THE ROCKS

Let the rivers clap their hands. Let the mountains sing together for joy.
—PSALM 98:8

Once, as Jesus traveled to Jerusalem, a crowd of people gathered around Him and began shouting out praises for all the miracles they had seen Him do. But the Pharisees didn't like this, and they wanted Jesus to tell the people to be quiet. But Jesus said, "I tell you . . . if they keep quiet, the stones will cry out" (Luke 19:40 NIV).

Jesus can make even the rocks and stones sing His praises—and that seems to be exactly what's happening just a few miles outside of Butte, Montana, where an unusual rock formation has people listening to the songs of the "Ringing Rocks." When someone strikes these special rocks with a hammer, the rocks ring like a bell. The shape of the rocks, their size, and how they are stacked cause each rock to produce a different sound.

Scientists aren't sure exactly why these rocks ring. They think perhaps it's because the rocks have iron in them. But Christians know the real reason: the rocks ring because God *created* them to ring. The Bible tells us in Psalm 19:1 that "the heavens tell the glory of God. And the skies announce what his hands have made"—and so do the animals, the trees, the oceans, and every single thing God has created. They all declare God is awesome and He is our Creator. Even the rocks ring out with His praises!

Lord, I cannot even count all the things I should praise You for—but I want to try! Help me remember to ring out Your praises every day.

BE AMAZED

A similar field of "Ringing Rocks" lies in Pennsylvania. In June of 1890, Dr. John J. Ott gathered enough of the special rocks (each rock weighing some 200 pounds) and arranged them according to their musical sounds. He then played a concert—a *real* rock concert—by hitting the stones with a steel hammer.

14

NO KIDDING

You are young, but do not let anyone treat you as if you were not important. Be an example to show the believers how they should live. Show them with your words, with the way you live, with your love, with your faith, and with your pure life.

—1 TIMOTHY 4:12

You probably know that a kitten grows up to be a cat, a puppy grows up to be a dog, and a duckling grows up to be a duck. But did you know that a *kit* grows up to be a fox? A *puggle* grows up to be a platypus? A *flapper* becomes a swan? Or a *fry* grows up to be a fish?

The real question, though, is what will *you* grow up to be? Will you become the person God designed you to be? God has given you special gifts and talents—things you can do that no one else can do in the same wonderful way. He wants you to use your gifts to love Him and love others. Loving God and loving others are the two greatest commandments, and you can find them in Matthew 22:37–40.

BE AMAZED

Kids can make a big difference in the world by doing little things—like comforting a friend, sharing what you have, or telling others about God. What can you do today to grow into the person God made you to be?

The great news is you don't have to wait until you're all grown up to start using your gifts and following God's Word. You can start right now. *But I'm just a kid*, you might say. That's okay—just check out what one kid in the Bible did. Josiah was only *eight years old* when he became king and led the people back to God. (Read about Josiah in 2 Kings 22–23.)

Now, you don't have to be a king to do what's right and to lead people to God. You can be a teacher, a firefighter, the president—or a kid. Just love God with all your heart, soul, and mind, and love others—and you'll grow up doing great things!

Dear God, thank You for creating me uniquely and with a purpose. Help me see all the ways—big and small—I can show Your love to others today.

15

GREAT BALLS OF FIRE!

God did not give us a spirit that makes us afraid. He gave us a spirit of power and love and self-control.
—2 TIMOTHY 1:7

The Sun—it warms our faces and gives light to our days. We also draw pictures of it: a small, bright-yellow ball with a smiley face in the center. It just seems so . . . friendly.

But that's *only* because the Sun is 93 million miles away!

Up close, our Sun isn't very friendly at all. It's a raging inferno of flames. The temperature of the Sun's core is 27 million degrees Fahrenheit! And it isn't some small, yellow ball either. It's huge—ginormously huge! If Earth were the size of a golf ball, the Sun would be about the size of an elephant.

God breathed that Sun out of His mouth (check out Psalm 33:6). What does that tell us about God? He is mighty. He is awesome. He is able to do things we cannot even begin to imagine. Our God is *ferocious* in His power!

What does God do with all that power? He gives His power to *you*. When you are tired of trying to do the right thing and getting nowhere, when your worries make you afraid to take a step, or when you feel attacked by troubles too big to handle on your own, don't be scared. Be bold! Be brave! Call out to God in prayer, and ask Him for His power. He *will* answer. And His Spirit will make you strong and mighty and powerful. Trust God. He is *ferociously* on your side, and He's got this.

Lord, I will never look at the Sun quite the same way. Your power is awesome! Thank You for loving me so much that You use the same power that breathed out the Sun to help me.

BE AMAZED

How big is the Sun? You could fit close to 1 million Earths inside the Sun. That would be like filling two entire school buses with golf balls!

16

THICK AND THIN

"I am the vine, and you are the branches. If a person remains in me and I remain in him, then he produces much fruit. But without me he can do nothing."

—JOHN 15:5

Let's start with an assignment: go stare at a tree. Don't just glance at it. *Really* study it. Examine its trunk, its color, and its branches. How tall is it? How wide?

A tree is one of God's greatest designs. In fact, in the book of Genesis, God Himself said it was a good design. Want to know something incredible? God repeated the basic design of a tree inside you—and in more ways than one.

You see, God created trees to have a main trunk and lots of branches that . . . well . . . *branch* off from the trunk. Those branches carry sap (which is kind of like a tree's blood) and its nutrients to every part of the tree.

God created your blood vessels to work in a similar way. These vessels carry your blood—and all its nutrients—to every part of your body. The biggest vessels connect to the heart and are like the trunk of a tree. The smaller vessels—like branches of a tree—branch off to carry blood into tinier and tinier areas, so every part of your body is reached.

In much the same way, Jesus is our divine tree, and we are branches growing from Him. If our connection to Him is damaged, then we are damaged too. Just as a branch cut away from a tree no longer grows or produces fruit, if we cut ourselves away from Jesus, we no longer grow or produce His fruit of love, kindness, joy, and peace.

BE AMAZED

The tallest tree in the world is a coast redwood tree. It's located in a remote part of Redwood National Park in California. Stretching an amazing 379.7 feet tall, it's been named *Hyperion*. By the way, that's about the height of a 35-story building—and even taller than most Ferris wheels!

So stay connected to Jesus—and you'll stay nourished and able to produce a rich harvest of heavenly fruit.

Thank You, Lord, for nourishing me like the branch of a tree. Help me always to stay connected to You, so I can keep growing and producing good fruit. You are all I need!

17

EARS TO HEAR

Don't just listen to God's word.
You must do what it says.
—JAMES 1:22 NLT

Your ears are an amazing creation. They not only allow you to hear, but they also help with balance and—believe it or not—with taste. Your ears never stop working, even when you are sound asleep.

Your ears work by capturing sound waves in the outer ear, which is called the *pinna*. That's the part of the ear you can see. Sound waves funnel down into the middle ear, where they turn into vibrations, and then they travel to the

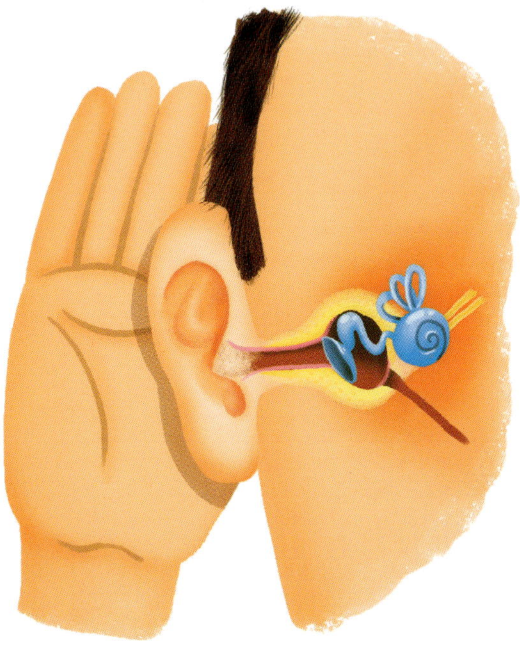

eardrum. From there, they flow into the cochlea, which is located in the inner ear. Next, the sound waves go to the brain—which puts everything together and tells you what you're hearing.

Your hearing is a great gift from God, but what you *do* with what you hear is your gift back to God. Jesus said it this way:

> "Everyone who hears these things I say and obeys them is like a wise man. The wise man built his house on rock. It rained hard and the water rose. The winds blew and hit that house. But the house did not fall, because the house was built on rock. But the person who hears the things I teach and does not obey them is like a foolish man. The foolish man built his house on sand. It rained hard, the water rose, and the winds blew and hit that house. And the house fell with a big crash." (Matthew 7:24–27)

Don't let your life come crashing down like that foolish man's house. Listen to God! How? Through reading His Word, through listening as others teach it, and through listening to the Holy Spirit as He reminds you of the things God has said. And after you listen to God's Word? Do what it says!

Lord, help me hear what Your Word teaches—and then give me the strength and bravery to do what it says.

BE AMAZED

Three bones make up the ear: the *malleus, incus,* and *stapes*. These are also known as the hammer, anvil, and stirrup. They are the smallest bones in the human body—so small that all three of them could fit on a single penny.

18

PACKED WITH POWER

You should know that your body is a temple for the Holy Spirit. The Holy Spirit is in you. You have received the Holy Spirit from God.
—1 CORINTHIANS 6:19

Ants are tiny little creatures, but they can lift up to 50 times their own weight. The rhinoceros beetle can lift something that's up to 100 times its weight. That would be like a person lifting something that weighs about 9 tons.

Or think of it this way—a polar bear weighs about half a ton, so it would be like lifting 18 polar bears. Even more impressive is the dung beetle, which can pull up to 1,141 times its body weight—and you don't want to think about what that dung beetle is pulling!

God can pack a lot of power and strength into tiny little packages. In fact, He packs an unbelievable amount of power and strength inside you. You see, when you decide to follow God and become one of His children, He packs His Spirit—the Holy Spirit—inside *you*. Your body actually becomes a home to the Spirit of God! That is an indescribable gift, but it is also a huge responsibility.

BE AMAZED

The webs of the Nephila orb-weaver spider are so strong that people in the South Pacific use them as fishing nets.

You see, this gift of the Holy Spirit wasn't free. "You were bought by God for a price" (1 Corinthians 6:20), and God paid that price when His Son, Jesus, suffered and died on the cross. As a result, God expects you to take extra good care of your body. That means eating good foods, exercising, and getting plenty of rest. It means not hurting yourself with drugs, alcohol, or smoking. But it's not enough just to watch what you put into your body. Honoring God also means not using your body to sin. This means avoiding things like using your mouth to gossip or letting your eyes watch things you shouldn't.

As a child of God, your body is packed with the power, strength, and presence of God's Spirit. Ask Him to help you use your body to honor Him and do what He wants you to do!

God, I know I am still kind of small, but I also know You can still use me in powerfully big ways. How can I live for You today?

19

ASTRONOMICAL GRACE

Those who are in Christ Jesus are not judged guilty.
—ROMANS 8:1

When I look up at the stars and think about how *huge* space is—so astronomically huge that scientists have never even glimpsed the edges of it—I feel a bit, well, *tiny*. But then I think about how amazing it all is and how amazing that means God is. *He made all of it!* And even more amazing is the fact that the One who made everything also loves you and me.

Proof of God's love and grace is all around us. It's as if all of creation is God's way of saying, "I love you." Don't believe it? Just look at what's inside the heart of the Whirlpool Galaxy.

The Whirlpool Galaxy lies some 30 million light-years away, and tucked inside it is something called the X-Structure. Scientists tell us the dark *X* marks the exact spot of a black hole so big that its size is equal to 1 million of our Suns. It's so *astronomically* big that it's 1,100 light-years across. That *is* amazing, but I believe the

X marks the spot of something more than just a black hole. Because if you tilt your head just a bit, that *X* looks just like a cross—and it marks the spot of yet another reminder of God's astronomical love and grace.

You see, God sent Jesus to Earth to live and die on a cross. Why? So your sins could be forgiven, and you could be with God. That's called grace. And no matter what you've done—no matter what mistake, what sin, what mess you've made—God is ready to forgive you. You just have to ask. Because God's grace isn't just big. It isn't just huge. It's *astronomical*!

Lord, sometimes I feel as if I've messed everything up. Thank You, Lord, for Your astronomical grace that forgives and covers even my biggest sins.

BE AMAZED

A black hole, which forms when a star is dying, is a place in space where the gravity is so strong that even light cannot escape. Since no light can escape black holes, they are invisible. Scientists can see them only by using special telescopes.

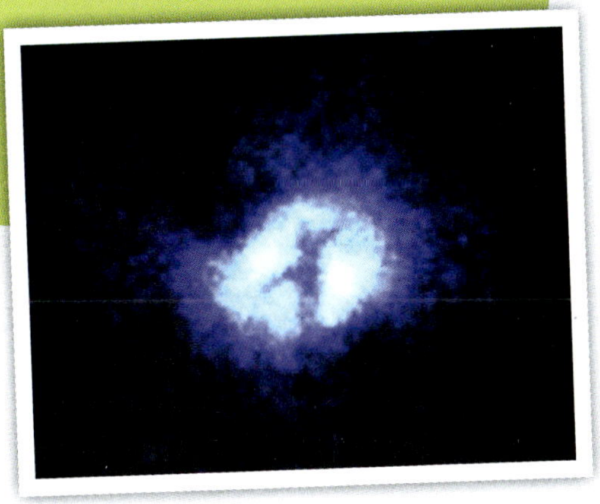

20

MOUNTAIN CLIMBING

I will pray to the Lord. And he will answer me from his holy mountain.
—PSALM 3:4

Mount Everest is the highest mountain in the world. Because it soars to a height of 29,029 feet above sea level (that's about 5½ miles), you would need to stack more than 20 Empire State Buildings—one of the tallest skyscrapers in the United States—on top of each other to equal its height.

Thousands of people have tried to climb Mount Everest, but not everyone can make it to the top. The cold and the lack of oxygen at the higher altitudes make climbing Everest extremely difficult. Climbers use experienced guides called *Sherpas* to help them know which trail to follow and to help them survive.

Have you ever felt as if you had a problem that was as big as Mount Everest? Maybe it's a problem with schoolwork, a problem at home, an illness, or something you just don't know how to handle. The good news is you have a guide to help you over that mountain of a problem—God—and He holds the record for being the best mountain climber around. In fact, the Bible says He already knows every single mountain you will face throughout your life, and He knows the perfect way to climb them. He'll show you which trail to follow, and He'll give you everything you need to survive. Just ask Him: a simple prayer is all it takes. He will answer—through the words of the Bible, through the advice of a trusted teacher or friend, or through His voice that whispers to your heart. Trust God with your troubles, and He'll guide you to the top.

Lord, sometimes my problems seem bigger than Mount Everest. Thank You for always being there to guide me when I need help, and even when I think I don't.

Mauna Kea

BE AMAZED

Mount Everest reaches the highest point of any mountain on Earth, but it's not actually the tallest. Mauna Kea, an inactive volcano in Hawaii, is the world's tallest mountain. It is only 13,796 feet above sea level, but it stretches almost 20,000 feet below the water. Its full height—from its base on the ocean floor to its top—is 32,696 feet!

21

SOMEBODY'S WATCHING YOU

He will not let you be defeated. He who guards you never sleeps. . . . The Lord will guard you as you come and go, both now and forever.
—PSALM 121:3, 8

Have you ever heard the saying, "Somebody's watching you"? Well, when you look at the Hourglass Nebula, you might say that's true! It's as if the eye of God is watching you and me!

Located about 8,000 light-years from the Earth, the Hourglass Nebula was formed by a dying star. The star ejected some of its outer layers and then flung these materials out into space on the stellar winds—giving it the hourglass look. That's what the scientists say anyway, but if you ask me . . . the Hourglass Nebula looks like a gigantic eyeball floating in space! And it reminds me that God is always watching over us.

Some people think the fact that God is always watching is a bad thing. They seem to think God is just waiting for us to mess up, so He can pounce on us. Nothing could be less true! Yes, God sees when you mess up. After all, He knows and sees everything—even before you think or do something. But nothing you do will ever make Him love you more, and no sin you commit will ever make Him love you less.

God is always watching—not to punish—but to protect and help. He never gets tired, and He never sleeps. He's always ready to help you, and He always has time to listen, no matter what time it is! Ask God to guide you and watch over you—He's not sleeping anyway.

God, You know all things, and you know all about me. You always see me, and You never stop protecting and leading me! You love me and want to help me. That is amazing to me, God. It's so amazing that it's . . . indescribable!

BE AMAZED

In the eighth century, a French monk named Liutprand invented the first hourglass (also called a sand clock). It measured time by the falling of sand from one glass bulb to the other. As early as the fourteenth century, sailors used the hourglass to tell time because the rolling waves did not affect it.

22

LIGHT UP THE WORLD

"You should be a light for other people. Live so that they will see the good things you do. Live so that they will praise your Father in heaven."

—MATTHEW 5:16

If you have ever seen the northern lights, then you know God can put on a light show like no other! The northern lights—or *aurora borealis*—are brightly colored lights that shimmer and dance across the sky in the areas around the North Pole. They are caused by fast-moving particles from the Sun (called solar wind) hitting the electromagnetic field that surrounds and protects the Earth from the Sun's most harmful rays. When those particles hit gas atoms in our atmosphere, those gases glow, creating a spectacular light show. The lights are so vivid they can even be seen from space.

BE AMAZED

The colors of the northern lights are created when the solar winds bump into different gases in the atmosphere. Yellow, red, and green come from bumping into oxygen. Violet and blue are created by the solar winds bumping into nitrogen.

Such an amazing show could only be created by an amazing God. And that light show's chief purpose is to tell us how great and glorious our God is.

But the sky isn't the only thing God uses to tell about His greatness and glory. God shines the light of His love into our lives and makes us glow with love for Him and for others. He fills us with His light for a great purpose—to shine into the world and show other people the way to follow Him.

How do we shine God's light? God says it this way: "Do not be bitter or angry or mad. Never shout angrily or say things to hurt others. Never do anything evil. Be kind and loving to each other. Forgive each other just as God forgave you in Christ" (Ephesians 4:31–32). When you live this way, you'll certainly light up the world!

God, light up my life with the light of Your love. Help me shine Your light into the whole world.

23

REST IN THE SHADE

**The Lord protects you as the shade
protects you from the sun.**
—PSALM 121:5

More than 28 million light-years away is a giant hat. Okay, so it's actually a galaxy that looks like a hat—a sombrero, to be exact. The galaxy's unusual appearance comes from a ring of dark dust around it and a bulge of billions of glowing stars in its center. Scientists believe a supermassive black hole—with the mass of 1 *billion* suns—lies at the center of the sombrero.

The word *sombrero* comes from the Spanish word *sombra*, which means "shade." In Mexico, the brim of sombreros can be as wide as 2 feet! That's a lot of shade, but it's needed. The sombrero's shade provides much-needed relief to a person working in the glaring heat of the Sun.

Sometimes, following Jesus can feel like hard work out in the scorching heat. You see, this world doesn't always want to hear about God, and it can "turn up the heat" when you try to tell people about Him. You might be laughed at for believing in God. People might say you can't pray in certain places or at certain times, or even talk about God out loud. And sometimes the things in your life are really hard—like when someone you love is sick, a person or pet dies, you're stressed out with schoolwork, or making friends seems difficult.

Sometimes you just need to rest in a bit of shade. God wants to be your shade, and He provides better protection than even the biggest sombrero. Take time to talk to Him and rest in His presence. He'll protect you and give you the rest you need—so you can go back out and face the heat of the world.

Lord, I want to tell the world all about You. But it's hard when people don't want to listen. Sometimes, the hard things in life make me tired and sad. Help me to rest in Your shade so I can go back out and tell more people about You.

BE AMAZED

The sombrero made its first appearance in the fifteenth century and was made of felt or straw. It was most popular in Spain, Mexico, and the southwestern United States. It was later adopted by ranchers and frontiersmen in the United States. Over time they turned the sombrero into the modern-day cowboy hat.

24

ALL CREATION SINGS

Praise the LORD from the heavens; . . . praise him, all you shining stars. . . . Praise the LORD from the earth, you great sea creatures and all ocean depths.
—PSALM 148:1, 3, 7 NIV

Everybody knows that stars twinkle and shine. But did you know that they also sing? All night long—and all day too—they sing out their praises to the One who hung them in the heavens and called them by name.

We know the stars sing because scientists have spent a lot of time listening to the heavens. Scientists aim large radio telescopes at the stars to capture their sounds. One star in particular, the Vela Pulsar, is about 1,000 light-years away. The Vela formed by exploding into a supernova as it was dying, and then it collapsed back in on itself with such force that it now rotates 11 times per second on its axis. (If that doesn't sound impressive, you try spinning 11 times per second!) As the Vela spins, it shoots out a radio frequency a rhythmic, drum-like beat that doesn't stop. And that's just one star!

BE AMAZED

Some stars beat out a steady *rat-a-tat-tat* beat. Others sing like violins. If you'd like to hear the stars' songs, ask your parents to help you search for a recording on the Internet.

Not only do the stars sing, but the whole Earth is in on the symphony. The trees clap, the mountains sing, and all the animals cry out, from the birds that chirp to the whale songs that echo across the oceans:

Our God is awesome and amazing.

Our God is mighty beyond our imagination.

Our God is *indescribable*!

All of creation sings God's praises because He created it all. But there's something about you that is different from the rest of creation—*God created you in His image.* God designed you to be like Him—so you have even more to sing about than the stars. Add your voice to God's symphony today!

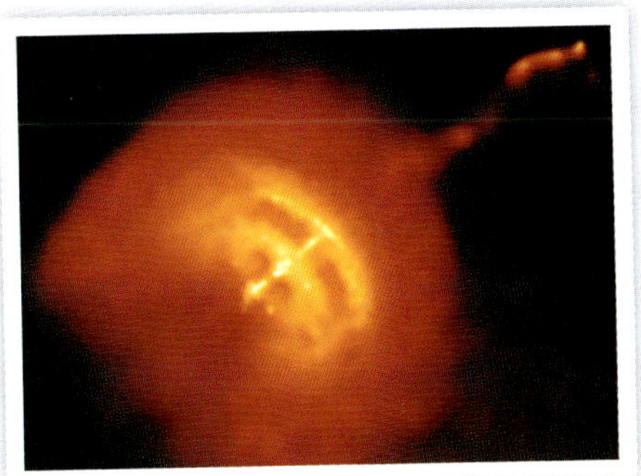

Vela Pulsar

Lord, You are so amazing. I want to add my voice to the songs of Your creation. I praise You for who You are and for all You have done. Your creation is incredible!

25

BUSY AS A . . . BEE?

By the seventh day God finished the work he had been doing. So on the seventh day he rested from all his work.

—GENESIS 2:2

Bees stay busy. Really busy. Just to fly, a bee has to flap its wings 200 times per second—which is what gives a bee its *bzzz* sound. The worker bees are the busiest of all. They're the ones that are sent out to find nectar and pollen, which they then turn into honey. *Entomologists*—that's a big word for "bug experts"—have found that bees make 12 collection trips each day. And a bee will visit between 50 and 100 flowers on each of those trips. These busy bees work almost nonstop from sunrise to sunset. And when they need a break, they may take a 30-second nap! Worker bees have very short but incredibly productive lives—the average worker bee lives only three to six weeks!

Of course, it's a good thing to work. It's good thing to play. And it's a good thing to be busy. But it's also a good thing to rest. Your body *needs* sleep. When you're asleep, your brain gets ready for the next day, tidying up thoughts and storing away things you want to remember. Sleep is also when your body heals and repairs your heart and blood vessels—to keep you running in tip-top shape. And when you're a kid, sleep is the time your body produces a hormone to help you grow. When you don't get enough sleep, you don't think clearly and your body doesn't work as well as it should. Even though God never gets tired (Psalm 121:4), He took time to rest after He created the world. He did that to teach us that rest is important. So, yes, go and be busy as a bee sometimes—but then make sure you get plenty of rest!

Lord, I understand there are times to be busy and times to rest. Teach me to work and to rest for Your glory.

Bee honeycomb

BE AMAZED

Honey is sometimes called a miracle food. That's because it contains almost every nutrient needed for life, and it won't spoil for years—even *thousands* of years. In fact, archaeologists have found pots filled with honey in ancient Egyptian tombs, and it's still good to eat!

26

SHINE ON

Try to shine as lights among the people of this world, as you hold firmly to the message that gives life.

—PHILIPPIANS 2:15–16 CEV

There's a lot of talk about moonlight and how it lights up the night. But, actually, there's no such thing as moonlight. The Moon doesn't really shine at all; rather, when it's in just the right place, the Moon reflects the Sun's light. The Sun is the real star of the show (no pun intended)! The Sun gives off light, which means it's *luminous*. But the Moon is *illuminated*, which means it's lit up by reflecting the Sun's light.

People are a lot like the Moon. *What? You mean round and spacey?* Not quite. But just as the Sun's light reflects into the darkness when the Moon is in just the right place, God's light also reflects into this world's sin-filled darkness when *you* are in the right place. Being in the right place means following Jesus. When you follow Jesus, you reflect His light—His love, goodness, grace, kindness, and power—into the lives of those around you. You shine simply by staying close to Him, the Light of the World!

But how? It's not difficult to do, although it does take practice. Study His Word, the Bible. Listen to those who teach about Him. And talk to Him in prayer every day. Your prayers don't have to be fancy, long, or eloquent. Say "thank you" when you see one of God's gifts. Tell Him that you love Him. Or simply whisper, "I don't know what to do, Lord. Help me." When you do this, you shine Jesus into the world.

BE AMAZED

On July 21, 1969, Neil Armstrong became the first man ever to walk on the Moon. He was part of NASA's Apollo 11 space mission. He stepped out of his spacecraft, the Eagle, and said, "That's one small step for man, one giant leap for mankind." And because the Moon has no wind, his footprints are still there!

God, help me stay close to You, so Your light always shines on me. And help me reflect Your light into the world.

27

I FEEL THE EARTH MOVE . . . UNDER MY FEET

Jesus Christ is the same yesterday, today, and forever.
—HEBREWS 13:8

Have you ever felt the Earth move under your feet—even when you weren't dancing? If so, you might have felt an earthquake!

We think of the Earth as being solid and still, but in reality, it's constantly on the move. The continents and oceans of our planet sit on tectonic plates that "float" on magma under the surface. The plates move and shift, sometimes bumping into each other and at other times drifting apart. One plate may slide on top of another, or two plates may crush against each other. When this happens, it creates a powerful force—and that force causes the Earth to shake, ripple, and crack. We call that an earthquake. Earthquakes can cause landslides, tsunamis, and flooding, but they can also create mountains and valleys. A really powerful earthquake can feel a lot like riding an out-of-control roller coaster—but a whole lot scarier!

Sometimes life feels as if you're stuck on a roller coaster. One minute everything is wonderful, and you're racing to the top. But the next minute, disaster strikes, and you're diving toward the bottom at a terrifying speed. Even though your life is constantly changing, God never changes. He is always working toward what's best for you—whether you're zooming up to the top, coasting through the middle, or plunging down to the bottom. In the middle of this ride, God holds on to you tightly. And He uses the ups and downs of this roller-coaster life to create mountains of faith and valleys of rest, shaping the course of your life with Him.

BE AMAZED

Did you know there are approximately 500,000 detectable earthquakes in the world every year? About 100,000 of them can actually be felt, but only about 100 cause any damage. Florida and North Dakota have the fewest earthquakes in the United States, while Alaska has the most, with as many as 4,000 per year!

God, when everything around me is zooming like a crazy roller coaster, I'm so thankful that You are with me. Always keep me safely strapped in with Your love.

28

TREASURES THAT LAST

"Don't store treasures for yourselves here on earth. . . . Store your treasure in heaven."
—MATTHEW 6:19–20

It's so easy to look at our world and think, "Wow! This place is huge!" And compared to our size, the Earth *is* huge. But compared to the rest of universe? Well, it's not so big after all.

Here are some facts for you: Imagine our entire solar system (that's the Earth, the Sun, the Moon, all the other seven planets and their moons) were the size of a quarter. That would make the Earth a microscopic speck of dust. The next nearest star, Proxima Centauri, would be another quarter that's two soccer fields away. If you were to compare our solar system to the entire Milky Way Galaxy, it would be a like putting a quarter on the United States. And that's compared to just one galaxy. Scientists think there are billions and billions of other galaxies in the universe.

With that perspective, Earth seems almost microscopic. And all those *things* we want—the newest gadget, the trendiest clothes—seem suddenly unimportant. That's because those things really are small compared to the vastness of God's universe. The treasures of Earth just don't last.

But there are things that do last and things that—even when compared to the vastness of the universe—are still important. They are the heavenly treasures that come from knowing and following God: love, joy, peace, patience, kindness, goodness, faithfulness, gentleness, and self-control. So the next time you find yourself worrying about earthly treasures, remember how small that stuff really is—and focus on heavenly treasures instead.

God, when I get caught up in wanting more and more stuff, remind me of what is really important and what will last forever. Help me focus on getting rich in the heavenly treasures that come from following You.

BE AMAZED

The bigger the mirror of a telescope, the farther we can see! The biggest ground telescope is the Gran Telescopio Canarias in the Canary Islands, with a mirror surface of 34 feet. It recently spotted a halo of stars 500 million light-years away! The Hubble Space Telescope can see even farther because it's out in space. It has a 7-foot-10.5-inch mirror and has photographed galaxies *billions* of light-years away!

Gran Telescopio Canarias

29

SON POWER

Jesus came to them and said, "All power in heaven and on earth is given to me."
—MATTHEW 28:18

If you had to go without food for a few days, you'd find it hard to do something even as simple as lifting your arm. Why? Because the energy

you get from food fuels your body to work. No food means no energy—and no waving your arm around.

Plants need food too. A plant's "food"—its energy—comes from the Sun. In fact, the Sun is the source of almost all of the Earth's energy and power. It warms our planet, it powers our weather, and it moves the waves and currents in our oceans. Life on Earth would be impossible without the Sun.

For every second of every minute of every day, the Sun converts almost 700 million tons of hydrogen gas into helium gas, and most of that turns into energy. Amazingly, we get more energy from the Sun in a single hour than what we need to power all the devices on our entire planet for a year!

There's another Son whose power is truly indescribable—God's only Son, Jesus. Jesus had the power to do impossible things, like heal the sick, make the blind see, raise the dead to life, and stop storms. Because of Jesus' power and because He gave His life for us, we receive forgiveness for our sins, the ability to talk with God, and the gift of living forever in heaven with Him. And with His power, Jesus helps *us* do things that seem impossible: to forgive someone who's hurt us, love our enemies, and do the right thing even when no one else is.

That's the power of the Son—and it shines brighter than a million Suns!

BE AMAZED

We usually think about our energy coming from fossil fuels, like oil and gasoline. We use the energy that comes from burning fossil fuels to run our cars, heat and cool our homes, and keep our stoves hot to cook meals. But fossil fuels are actually secondhand forms of solar energy. That's because fossil fuels are plants that have broken down over time. But even those plants started out with the energy of the Sun.

Jesus, sometimes doing the right thing seems impossible. But I know You will help me with Your power. Thank You for making the impossible possible.

30

THE WOW FACTOR

In all the work you are doing, work the best you can. Work as if you were working for the Lord, not for men.
—COLOSSIANS 3:23

Put down this book—just for a minute—and take a look outside the window. Whether you're in the country or city, whether it's night or day, God's creation is all around you. There are the big, huge, indescribably amazing things like the Sun, the Moon, the Milky Way, and the billion-jillion other wonders of the universe. And then there are the massive wonders of this Earth, like soaring mountains, rolling seas, and roaring lions.

God has certainly created some incredible—and incredibly big—things. But today, take a look at the little things. Examine the leaf on the tree, the delicate wings of a butterfly, or the perfection of a spider's web. Lift up your hand and trace the tiny ridges of your fingerprint—a fingerprint that God gave you and you alone. Our God doesn't just "wow" with the biggest things of His creation. He also "wows" with the attention He gives to even the littlest things.

And God wants you to do the same thing. God is an excellent Creator, and you can honor Him by doing everything in life with excellence. Don't just give your best efforts on the big projects, the big games, the big tests. Don't work hard only when someone else is watching. Give it your all, even in the ordinary, everyday stuff—from cleaning your room to riding the bench at the ballgame. Do your very best in all things, even when no one else notices. Because God notices. Do all things for God because Your work honors Him! That's what God calls being faithful in the little things. And when you're faithful in the little things, God knows He can trust you with the big things too (Luke 16:10).

Lord, help me honor You in the way I serve You in all things—big and little—as well as those things no one else ever notices. Thank You for Your attention to both the big and the small!

BE AMAZED

Here are some fascinating butterfly facts: Butterflies taste with their feet. A group of butterflies is called a *kaleidoscope*. The skipper butterfly is so fast, it can outpace a horse. And here's a gross one: many adult butterflies never poop—they use up everything they eat for energy.

31

WHEN STARS DIE

Again Jesus cried out in a loud voice. Then he died. Then the curtain in the Temple split into two pieces.
—MATTHEW 27:50–51

Stars are born, and they also die. We usually think of dying as an ugly thing, but when a star dies, it is actually quite beautiful.

Stars are basically big balls of gas. When that gas burns up, the star dies. Smaller stars shrink and become *white dwarves.* Eventually they stop shining completely and become *black dwarves.* Bigger stars produce iron as they burn. The iron soaks up the star's energy like a sponge until it explodes into a supernova—a stunningly beautiful thing to see.

When Jesus died on the cross, the suffering of His death would have been the most horrible thing to see—and the most beautiful. *Beautiful? How could Jesus' death be beautiful?* It was beautiful because of the reason He did it.

Jesus *chose* to die so we could be

saved from our sins. Jesus—the shining star of heaven—died in a supernova of grace so great that the temple curtain was torn in two. The curtain that separated the people from God was torn from top to bottom because God reached down from heaven and ripped it in two. And because Jesus died, you and I can stand in

front of God with all our sins washed away by the holiness of Jesus. And you and I—and all who choose to follow Him—will spend eternity in heaven with Him. Now that is truly beautiful.

Jesus, thank You for suffering on the cross because of my sins. It's hard to believe You did that for me. Thank You for Your beautiful gift. Help me live each day as a praise to You.

BE AMAZED

Before Jesus died on the cross, the temple curtain separated the people from the Holy of Holies, which is where the presence of God was. Because the people were sinful, they could not be in the presence of God. Only once a year could the high priest go behind the curtain—but only after lots of special cleansing and sacrifices were done to atone for (or pay for) the people's sins. Scholars believe the curtain was 60 feet high, 30 feet wide, and as much as 4 inches thick—a curtain only God could tear in two!

32

THE BEAUTY INSIDE

God began doing a good work in you.
And he will continue it until it is finished
when Jesus Christ comes again.
—PHILIPPIANS 1:6

Stalactite. Stalagmite. One grows up and one grows down. But which one is which? Here's a trick: there's a *c* in *stalactite,* which grows from the ceiling.

Stalactites and stalagmites are formations that grow inside limestone caves. When water flows down through the caves, it dissolves calcite (a part of the limestone) and carries it through cracks in the ceiling. The water drips down and leaves behind tiny bits of the calcite. Over years of dripping, the calcite collects on the ceiling and a stalactite slowly forms, looking like a rocky icicle.

As water drips down the stalactite to the cave floor, more calcite collects on the floor. This slowly forms into a stalagmite. That's why the two formations are usually found together. Sometimes they even grow together to form a single column. These hidden formations can be stunning in beauty—and I have to wonder how many of them go unseen in undiscovered caves.

Tucked inside the Earth, these stunning works of God's creation are made slowly over many years. In a similar way, God is creating an even more beautiful and stunning work inside you. Day by day, moment by moment, experience by experience, God is forming and shaping your heart . . . to look just like His. It's a work that takes time—all the years of your life, actually. But don't worry, God is patient, and He's promised that He'll keep working on you until you are made perfect in heaven.

Thank You for being patient with me, God. And when I mess up, help me remember that You're still working on me.

Cave of Crystals

BE AMAZED

Discovered by accident, the Cave of Crystals lies hidden 1,000 feet beneath the Naica Mine, which is located in the Chihuahua Desert in Mexico. It's a magical—and deadly—place. Temperatures inside the Cave of Crystals can soar to 118 degrees with 90 percent humidity, so a person inside it can die within 30 minutes without the protection of a special suit. Inside the cavern, which is the size of a football field, enormous towers of sparkling, white gypsum crystals sprout like icicles from the walls, the floor, and the ceiling—making it look like a real-world ice palace.

33

SEE THE SEAHORSE

I wait for the Lord to help me. I trust his word.

—PSALM 130:5

The seahorse (or Hippocampus, if you want to be scientific!) is a tiny fish that lives in the oceans. It's called a seahorse because its head looks like the head of—you guessed it—a tiny horse. This unusual creature often swims with another seahorse, and they link their tails to stay together. It also swims "standing up" and tries to blend in with nearby plants so it doesn't get eaten.

Because of its body shape, the seahorse isn't a very good swimmer. So rather than go out hunting for food, seahorses use their tails like anchors, holding on to a piece of sea grass or coral. They then wait for food—plankton and tiny crustaceans—to drift by so they can suck it up with their long snouts.

With its poor swimming and its tendency to stay in one spot, the seahorse isn't going to win any races. But God has given it everything it needs: a way to get food, someone to swim through life with, and something to hold on to. God promises the same to you. The Bible says, "God will use his wonderful riches in Christ Jesus to give you everything you need" (Philippians 4:19). God provides you with food and shelter, Jesus to swim through life with, and the promises of His Word to hold on to. Like the seahorse, you may sometimes have to hold on and wait for God to deliver His promises—but He always will, and at just the perfect time.

Help me, Lord, to wait for Your perfect timing. And while I wait, teach me to live the way You want me to. I will follow You!

BE AMAZED

Seahorses are one of the few animals for which the male bears the young for the female. A female seahorse lays her eggs—sometimes hundreds of them—in a pouch on the male seahorse's tummy. The pouch is very much like a kangaroo's pouch. The eggs stay in the pouch until they hatch about 45 days later. A baby seahorse is only about the size of a jelly bean and must start finding its own food as soon as it's born.

34

BEETLE JUICE

Come near to God, and God will come near to you.
—JAMES 4:8

Betelgeuse—you pronounce it "beetle juice," which sounds like a nasty Halloween punch, doesn't it? Well, it's actually a star. Not just any twinkling little star, but a truly spectacular star that's approximately 640 light-years away from the Earth. Remember, a light-year is how far light travels in a year, which is 5.88 trillion miles! Multiply that by 640 and . . . well . . . let's just say Betelgeuse is farther away than anyone can really imagine. And it's so big that 262 trillion Earths could fit inside this massive star.

But Betelgeuse isn't the biggest star we know about. Another one, about 3,000 light-years away, is called Mu Cephei. It's a ferocious beast of a star. More than 2.7 *quadrillion* Earths would fit inside Mu Cephei. And by the way, a quadrillion is a 1 followed by 15 zeroes! That's a big star, but you know what's amazing? Even bigger stars exist in our universe, and we know God made billions more that we just haven't discovered yet.

BE AMAZED

Some numbers—like a quadrillion—are so big they're hard to understand. Think of it this way: 1 million seconds equals 12 days. A billion seconds is about 32 years. One trillion seconds is almost 30,000 years. And 1 quadrillion seconds? That equals 31,709,792 years!

To make stars that huge and far away, God must be bigger than anything you could imagine. But unlike the stars He made and hung in the skies, God's not far away at all. In fact, *He's right by your side*! He is with you, and He is everywhere all at the same time. It's called being *omnipresent*. That's a unique quality that only God has—a quality that makes Him *indescribable.*

Jesus made this promise in Matthew 28:20: "You can be sure that I will be with you always." All you have to do is call on His name and He'll come even closer—to love you, to help you, to take care of you. God's just indescribably awesome that way.

God, sometimes I feel very small in this gigantic universe You've made. But I love knowing that I'm important enough to You for You to stay right beside me.

35

A MIRACLE? YEP, THAT'S YOU!

So God created human beings in his image.
In the image of God he created them.
He created them male and female.
—GENESIS 1:27

Did you know you're a miracle? It's true! You are a crazy, amazing miracle. Even though you are so tiny compared to the vastness of this universe, you are created in the image of God. That's right! The God who breathes out fiery, ferocious stars and hangs them in the sky is the same One who crafted and created you. You are fearfully made "in an amazing and wonderful way" (Psalm 139:14).

You began in your mother's womb when God created a unique, never-before-seen guide for how He'd build you. Think of it like a blueprint, which is the guide builders use to construct a new building. Your blueprint is called DNA (deoxyribonucleic acid), and it contains all the information for how you look and function—from the color of your eyes and hair to the shape of your toenails. Your DNA describes exactly how God wanted you to be, and there's never been and never will be another DNA code (or blueprint) like it. In all the history—and future—of the human race, there's only one *you*.

Scientists have figured out that God's DNA code for you is 3 billion characters long. (A *character* is like a single letter or number.) And this DNA code is planted inside each cell of your body, so all the cells function and grow according to the same master plan. Your body has *37.2 trillion cells*—and they each follow God's grand design to make you exactly into who He planned you

to be before you were even born! Your hair, your eyes, and your smile are all exactly as God designed them to be. An amazing and wonderfully designed miracle called . . . *you*.

God, when I start to feel like I'm nobody special, remind me of who I really am—a marvelous miracle made by You!

BE AMAZED

Your DNA code is so long that if the DNA from just one cell were stretched out, it would be 6 feet long! If you stretched out the entire DNA in all 37.2 trillion of your cells, it would reach all the way to the moon and back. Not just once, but 150,000 times!

36

THE EYES HAVE IT

Open my eyes to see the wonderful things in your teachings.
—PSALM 119:18

Take a look around you for a second. What do you see? Lights and colors and movements and things both tiny and huge. Your eyes are an amazing gift from God. And He began making them when you were still in your mother's womb. When you were at about five months of development, 1 million *optic* (that's a fancy word for something that has to do with your eye) nerve endings stretched out from your brain to meet and match up with another million optic nerve endings that stretched out from your eye. All 2 million of them matched up perfectly! Can you imagine matching up 2 million different wires and getting them all exactly right? Yet that's exactly what God did when making your eyes. Even the most technologically advanced machine on the Earth is nothing compared to the magnificence of your eyes.

All that happened at five months of growth, but you still couldn't see a thing. Why? Because your eyeballs were covered with skin. But at about the sixth month, a miraculous and mysterious thing happened: the skin separated—giving you eyelids for the very first time. All while you were still in your mother's womb!

The God who created all the wonders of this world created your eyes to see those wonders, so you could praise Him. And the God who shared His words in the Bible gave you eyes to read them so you could obey Him. This world will try to show you all sorts of terrible things that aren't from God and sinful things that don't make Him smile. Look away! Look at God and His wonders instead.

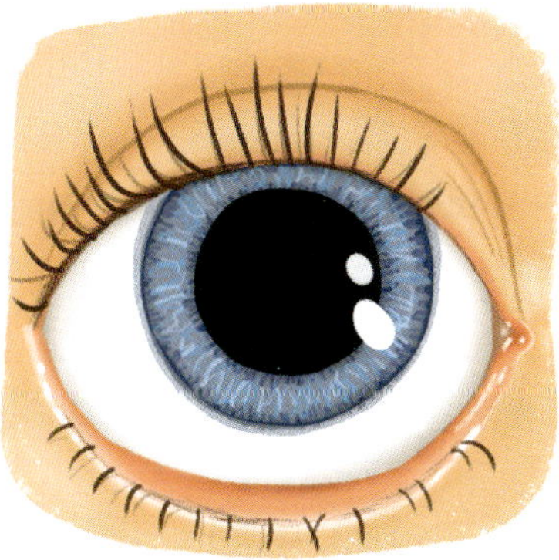

Lord God, thank You for the gift of my eyes. Open them to see all the gifts You have blessed me with—and help me thank You for every one!

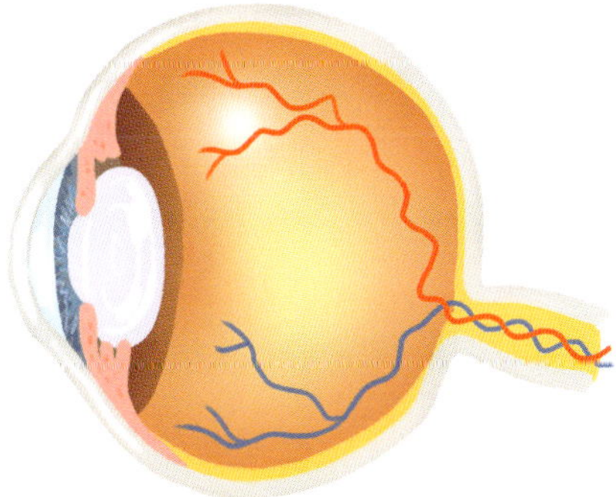

BE AMAZED

Chameleons have some of the coolest eyes around—and I do mean *around*. A chameleon can see in a total 360-degree circle—all the way around its body. That's because it doesn't have eyelids like humans do. Instead, it has a cone around each eye with a small opening for the pupil. And *each* eye can move separately from the other, so it can look in two different directions at once!

37

WHICH WAY TO GO?

Your word is like a lamp for my feet and a light for my way.
—PSALM 119:105

In the spring and fall, you've probably seen huge flocks of birds flying overhead. What are those guys up to? Every year, certain animals move from one place to another in huge groups. It's called *migration*.

Why do animals migrate? Usually it's to find food, get to warmer weather, or reach a safer place to have their babies. What scientists don't understand is *how* animals know when to move and where to go. Perhaps it's the changes in the weather or the length of the days that tell animals when it's time to

move. And perhaps they use the stars, the Sun, or even the wind patterns to figure out which way to go. Scientists say animals are just born knowing what to do—they call it *instinct*. But that's really just a fancy way of saying God tells the animals—His creation—what to do.

And He does the same thing for you . . . in a different way. When you don't know what to do or where to go or how to get there, God gives you the answers—and you can find them in His Word, the Bible. Some people turn to friends or family or other people when they don't know what to do. And that's okay, but remember that those people aren't perfect. You need to be sure to talk to God. Only He is perfect, and only His answers are always right.

Lord, when I don't know what to do, teach me to turn to You and to Your Word for the answers I seek. I know You will always show me the right way to go. Thank You for guiding me.

BE AMAZED

The Arctic tern holds the record for the longest migration. This little bird travels more than 43,000 miles every year from its nesting grounds in the Arctic to its winter home in Antarctica and then back again. It basically flies from one end of Earth to the other! Since an Arctic tern can live for more than 30 years, it can travel enough miles in its lifetime to go to the Moon and back again—almost three times!

38

A GIANT GOD

Who has measured the oceans in the palm of his hand?
—ISAIAH 40:12

Have you ever been to the ocean? The water stretches for miles and miles—as far as your eyes can see. How much water is there? Well, scientists have done the math, and they believe the Earth's oceans contain approximately 332,519,000 cubic miles of water. I know . . . a cubic mile is kind of confusing. But think of it this way: one mile is about the same length as 14 ⅔ football fields. So imagine a box that's 14 ⅔ football fields long, 14 ⅔ football fields wide, and 14 ⅔ football fields deep. Now fill that box with water—and that's *one* cubic mile of water. You would need 332,519,000 of those boxes to equal the water in our oceans! That's more boxes (and more water!) than I can imagine.

What does all that water have to do with God? Well, the Bible says He can measure the oceans in the palm of His hand. That's how big He is. Try scooping up some water in your hand. How much can you hold? A half of a cup? A fourth of a cup? God can hold much, much more than that. *God can scoop up all the water in all the oceans on the entire Earth and hold it in just one of His hands!*

God is a giant God, and compared to Him we are just teeny, tiny specks. But we aren't specks in His eyes. Every single person on Earth is important to God. We are so important that He sent His own Son, Jesus, to the Earth to save us from our sins—which are the things we do that are wrong (check out John 3:16). Because God is so big, we know that His love for each of us must be huge!

Lord, You are so big and I am so small, but You love me so much that You sacrificed Your own Son to save me. Thank You, God, for Your great big love.

BE AMAZED

All put together, the Earth's oceans cover more than 70 percent of the planet. The Pacific Ocean is the largest and covers about 30 percent of the Earth. The Atlantic Ocean is the second largest and covers about 20 percent of the Earth.

39

DANGER: POISON!

When you talk, do not say harmful things. But say what people need—words that will help others become stronger.
—EPHESIANS 4:29

Have you ever seen one of these cute little frogs? They mostly live in the tropical forests of Central and South America. God made them in a rainbow of brilliant colors: yellow, gold, copper, red, blue, green, and black—to name a few. But if you ever see one, watch out! They're not just cute; they're also deadly. Those bright colors are actually a warning sign to scare away would-be predators looking for a tasty snack. Native hunters in Colombia have used this frog's powerful poison for centuries, rubbing it on the tips of their blowgun darts—and that's how this cute little guy got its not-so-cute name: the poison dart frog. Just one of the golden frogs—the most deadly kind—has enough poison in its little body to kill ten men!

This frog certainly packs powerful poison. It's almost as powerful as *your* poison. What? *You* can be poisonous? It's true. You have a muscle—actually a group of muscles working together—that when used the wrong way can be more poisonous than a whole army of dart frogs. It's called your tongue.

God's Word says the tongue "is full of poison that can kill" (James 3:8). Your tongue is packed with the power to hurt and destroy—not just one person but lots of people if you don't keep it under control. But the good news is, your tongue has just as much power to build up and encourage, if you ask God for help! He'll take the poison out of your tongue and help you use it and your words to do good things—like telling other people about His love and caring for them. After all, God's words created life, so your words can bring His light and love to this world too!

Lord, teach me to be careful of what I say and never to use my words to hurt others. Instead, help me use my words to tell others about Your love.

BE AMAZED

In some countries, if you stick your tongue out at someone, people might think you're being silly—or incredibly rude. You could get a good laugh—or you could get in *a lot* of trouble. But in Tibet, a region in China, you'd simply be saying, "Hello!"

40

A HAIRY SITUATION

"When five sparrows are sold, they cost only two pennies. But God does not forget any of them. Yes, God even knows how many hairs you have on your head. Don't be afraid. You are worth much more than many sparrows."

—LUKE 12:6–7

Hair—it's everywhere! It's on your head and on your skin. It makes up your eyebrows and your eyelashes. It even grows in your ears and in your nose! In fact, the only places hair doesn't grow are on the palms of your hands, the bottoms of your feet, and your lips. Hair isn't just for looks either. It has a purpose. The hair on your head helps keep you warm. Eyelashes keep dust and dirt out of your eyes, while eyebrows help keep the sweat and rain away—not to mention helping you look shocked and surprised! And those nose and ear hairs help keep germs, pollen, and other bits of stuff out of your body.

Hair grows out of a special organ under your skin called a *follicle*. The average person has 100,000 follicles on his head—and more than 5 million on the entire body. That's a lot of hair! And God knows each and every hair in each and every follicle! You might not be able to count them all, but He can. The Bible tells you so.

When you're going through a tough time, especially if it's a *long*, tough time, you may start to feel that God has forgotten you. But that's not true. God could *never* forget you. Jesus said God knows what happens to every tiny bird in His world. And He loves you a lot more than any bird! When tough times come, God doesn't forget you, and you're not alone. God is always with you, even though you may not see it. Remember, the God who knows every hair on your head also knows exactly how to take care of you.

Lord, You know everything that happens in my life—even how many hairs are on my head! So I'll always trust You to do what's best for me.

BE AMAZED

Hair is one of the main characteristics of mammals (and people are mammals too). In fact, all mammals have hair or fur. Even naked mole rats have tiny hairs on their feet!

41

FOLLOW THE LEADER

"I am the good shepherd. I know my sheep, and my sheep know me."
—JOHN 10:14

Did you know people are sheep? That's what the Bible says . . . well . . . sort of. The Bible often says that we're like sheep and Jesus is the Good Shepherd. As it turns out, sheep really need a shepherd—just as we really need our Shepherd.

Why do sheep need a shepherd? Let's take a look at some facts about these fuzzy fellows. First of all, there are lots of sheep—more than one billion in the world. A group of sheep is called a *herd*, a *flock*, or a *mob*. Sheep frighten easily (kind of like us sometimes), so they like to stick together. This helps them feel secure and protects them from predators like wolves. Sheep also like to follow the crowd—even if it isn't a good idea. (Hmm . . . sound familiar?) They've even been known to follow their leader sheep right off a cliff. So sheep need a shepherd to keep them going in the right direction.

How are we like sheep? Well, don't we like to stick with the crowd? Don't we often do what everyone else is doing—even if it's not a good idea? That's why we need the Good Shepherd to keep us headed in the right direction.

Another interesting fact about sheep is that they can recognize faces—up to fifty different ones. That means sheep know their shepherd because they spend time with him and trust him to take care of them. In that way, we *should* be like sheep. We should spend so much time with our shepherd that we know Him and trust Him to take care of us. So as little sheep, we should follow our Leader.

Jesus, thank You for always watching over me. I want to know You better each day. Please give me the courage to follow wherever You lead me.

BE AMAZED

Jesus is the Good Shepherd in John 10, and stories of other shepherds are all throughout the Bible. Abel, the son of Adam and Eve, was the very first shepherd. Joseph and his brothers were shepherds. Moses was a shepherd before he led the Israelites out of Egypt. So was King David—before he became king, of course. And when Jesus was born, some of His first visitors were shepherds.

42

PALMING THE PLEIADES

"Can you tie up the stars of the Pleiades? Can you loosen the ropes of the stars in Orion? Can you bring out the stars at the right times?"
—JOB 38:31–32

What can you hold in the palm of your hand? Can you hold a golf ball, a tennis ball, or a baseball? Some professional basketball players' hands are so big they can hold a basketball! They call it *palming* the ball. But that's nothing compared to God. He can *palm* the Pleiades.

But what are the Pleiades, you ask? The Pleiades is a star cluster—a group of stars so big and bright that they can be seen from just about anywhere on Earth without binoculars or a telescope. They are more than 443 light-years away—that's 2,604 trillion miles! And our God can hold the entire Pleiades in the palm of His hand. In fact, the Bible tells us He can measure the whole universe with just His hand (Isaiah 40:12).

Do you know what else God holds in His hands? *You*. God, who is powerful enough to hold the whole universe, also holds you in His hands. And He loves you so much that nothing—no problem, no worry, no bully, no bad day—can ever snatch you out of His hand (John 10:28). Oh, the devil will try. He'll throw all kinds of yucky stuff at you, and he'll tempt you to do things you know you shouldn't do. But God is bigger and stronger, and the devil is no match for Him. So hang on to God. Talk to Him, listen to Him, and read about Him in His Word. And, remember, God's also holding on to you—and He won't let go.

Lord, if You can hold the whole universe in the palm of Your hand, I know I can trust You to hold on to me. Thank You for holding me in Your hands.

BE AMAZED

Scientists think 3,000 stars are in the Pleiades star cluster, but without a really powerful telescope, we can see only about 6 or 7 of the brightest ones. In ancient times, sailors used these bright stars to help them navigate their ships through the oceans.

43

BEAUTIFUL AND UNBREAKABLE

We are pressed on every side by troubles, but we are not crushed.
—2 CORINTHIANS 4:8 NLT

Nothing sparkles like a diamond. But they aren't just pretty to look at; diamonds are also the hardest natural substance known to man. In fact, the word *diamond* comes from a Greek word that means "unbreakable." Only another diamond can make a scratch on a diamond. They're so tough that they're sometimes used in tools for cutting, grinding, and drilling. Diamonds are rare and expensive because they form only under very special conditions.

A diamond is made from pure carbon, like graphite (which is your pencil lead) . But in order for a diamond to form, extreme pressures and incredibly hot temperatures are needed over a long period of time. This usually happens at about 100 miles below the Earth's crust—so volcanoes make good diamond "factories." When the volcanoes erupt, the diamonds "shoot" up toward the Earth's surface.

So . . . in a very dark place, under a lot

of pressure and stress and heat . . . something beautiful and unbreakable forms. Have you ever been in a dark place? Under a lot of pressure and stress? Could it be that God was using that time to make something beautiful and unbreakable? When you feel as if you're being pressed on every side by trouble, don't give up. God won't let you be crushed. He'll use those hard times to make you stronger and to teach you to depend on Him. Trust Him, especially when it's hard. He's making something beautiful and unbreakable—your faith in Him.

Lord, when I feel pressed down by my troubles, help me remember You already have an answer all figured out. Please give me strength while I learn to trust You to make me into something beautiful that reflects Your glory.

BE AMAZED

A *carat* is used to measure how much a diamond weighs. One carat equals 200 milligrams—or about the same as a raindrop. The biggest diamond ever found was the Cullinan Diamond, found in 1905 in a mine in South Africa. It was 3,106 carats—that's 1⅓ pounds, or about the same weight as a guinea pig! The diamond was cut into about 100 pieces, with the biggest piece called the Great Star of Africa. It is 530 carats and is mounted in the Royal Scepter of Britain.

44

TASTE AND SEE

Taste and see that the Lord is good.
—PSALM 34:8 NLT

Taste—we taste with our tongues, at least mostly. But some of God's creations are a lot more . . . well . . . *interesting* than that. For instance, a butterfly tastes with its feet, while a fly tastes with both its lips *and* its feet. Bees taste with their mouthparts, their front legs, and their antennae. An octopus tastes with the suckers of its tentacles—and some species of octopus have as many as 1,800 suckers! But the earthworm tops them all: its entire body is covered with taste buds. (Of course, since an earthworm pretty much just moves

through dirt, who knows how great that taste would be?)

We, however, taste primarily with our tongues, although our noses can get involved a little bit too. We have somewhere between 3,000 and 10,000 taste buds on our tongues. The things we taste fall into five different categories: sweet, sour, salty, bitter, and savory. (Another word for savory is *umami*.)

All these taste buds are an important part of God's design for us. Our sense of taste protects us by helping us avoid eating things that are rotten or poisonous or just plain bad for us. But God also gave us a sense of taste so we could experience foods that taste good too. Think of your favorite food: Can you imagine how delicious it tastes? God fills our world with blessings and signs of His goodness, and He *wants* us to enjoy them. God wants us to open up all our senses to experience the wonders of His creation. Taste and see—and touch and hear and smell—that God is good, and He creates good things!

BE AMAZED

The giraffe's tongue is more than 1½ feet long, which means it can lick its entire face! Cats and dogs use their tongues to clean their fur and remove fleas or other parasites. *Blech!* Chameleons, anteaters, and frogs use their sticky tongues to catch their lunch of bugs. *Double blech!*

Lord, open my eyes to see Your creation, my nose to smell Your flowers, and my ears to hear Your songs in nature. Help me touch others with Your love. Thank You for all the good things You give me. I love being Your child!

45

SHOOTING DOWN THE BIG BANG

Every house is built by someone, but God is the builder of everything.
—HEBREWS 3:4 NIV

This may come as a surprise, but not everyone believes God created the universe. Some people believe it just sort of . . . happened, all by itself. They believe the whole ginormous universe began as a tiny, hot mass of matter just a few millimeters in size. That tiny mass exploded out into what they call the Big Bang—an explosion so huge and so fast that it created the entire universe in a split second.

Some people also believe that life began by *evolution*. They claim when the Big Bang created the Earth, there were certain chemicals in the water. These chemicals—proteins, amino acids, and such—sort of sloshed around in a kind of soup. Lightning hit the soup just right, and the first cells of life suddenly sprang into being. After a long time and a lot more evolution, these cells grew and changed until they became plants and trees, puppies, elephants, eagles, crocodiles, and you and me.

I think the Big Bang was actually when light went zip-zapping across the universe after God said, "Let there be light!" (Genesis 1:3). And unlike slow evolution, creation was probably pretty noisy with all the roaring and chirping after God made birds, fish, and animals of every kind (Genesis 1:20–26). And when God said He'd like some people too, some praising from Adam and Eve added to the sounds.

BE AMAZED

Evolution says everything just sort of fell perfectly into place to create life. Try this experiment: Grab a puzzle—it doesn't matter how many pieces—and toss the pieces into the air. Did they put themselves together? No? Try again . . . and again. Still not right? If a simple puzzle can't put itself together, how can 37.2 trillion cells of a person put themselves together without someone putting them in just the right place?

Every type of creation—every great painting, building, and book—has a creator. Life, the Earth, and the universe are no different. It wasn't some huge cosmic accident, and neither are you. You are part of the creation of the grandest Creator of all—God!

Lord, Your creation is so amazing and so detailed—I know it wasn't just some accident. Thank You for creating me to be a part of it!

46

JUST BREATHE

The people who trust the Lord will become strong again. They will be able to rise up as an eagle in the sky. They will run without needing rest. They will walk without becoming tired.

—ISAIAH 40:31

Breathing—it's something you do every day, all day long, whether you're awake or asleep. When you breathe in air, which is full of oxygen, it travels in through your nose (or your mouth, if your nose is stuffy!) and into your lungs. Your lungs send the oxygen from the air to every cell of your body to give them energy. As your cells use the oxygen, they make a waste gas called carbon dioxide. That's what you breathe out.

Your brain actually tells you how fast to breathe. When you exercise or get frightened or get excited, your cells need more energy—and thus more oxygen. So your brain tells your lungs to breathe faster. But when you're asleep, you don't need as much energy, and your brain tells your lungs to slow down.

Breathing isn't something you really have to think about, though. Aren't you glad God made your body that way? But sometimes, it gets hard to breathe. Have you ever faced a problem so big that it felt hard to breathe? Or have you ever been so frightened or felt so lonely that you just couldn't seem to catch your breath?

When it gets hard to breathe, stop everything and go to God. Pray and tell Him everything you're feeling. Then just sit quietly with Him. He'll help you catch your breath. And then He'll give you the strength to take the next breath, and then the next one, and then one more. God won't let go of you—not

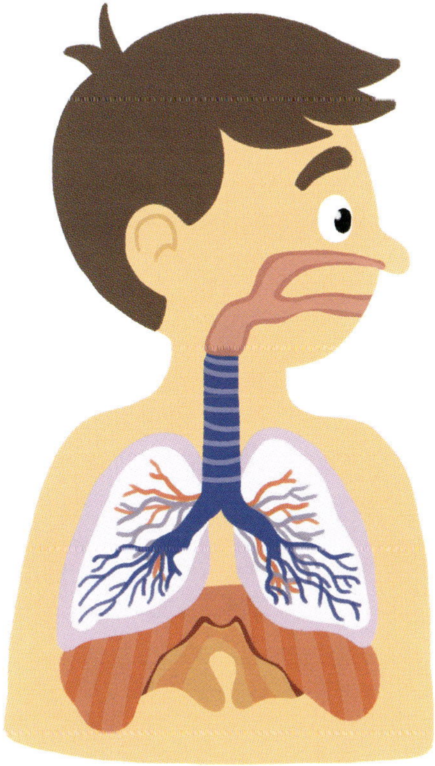

ever. And He'll bring you safely through whatever trouble you're facing. That's not just a promise—it's *God's* promise to *you*. And God never goes back on His promises!

Lord, when the stuff that's happening around me makes it hard to breathe, I'm so grateful I can come to You and find rest—and a chance to breathe again.

BE AMAZED

The average person can hold his or her breath for 30 seconds. But the Guinness world record belongs to Aleix Segura Vendrell. He held his breath for 24 minutes and 3.45 seconds in Barcelona, Spain, in February 2016. Now that's some lung power!

47

STAYING GROUNDED

All Scripture is inspired by God and is useful to teach us what is true and to make us realize what is wrong in our lives. It corrects us when we are wrong and teaches us to do what is right.
—2 TIMOTHY 3:16 NLT

Gravity is a force that pulls two objects together—it's what keeps your feet pulled down to the ground. Gravity might not seem like a big deal, *until* you think about life without it. It's the Earth's gravity that keeps you from floating off into space, and it's what makes an apple fall off a tree—just ask Isaac Newton about that one!

Gravity also affects how much you weigh, because weight is a measurement of how much gravity pulls on an object. For example, you would weigh a tiny bit less at the equator than at the North Pole because gravity has a slightly stronger pull at the North Pole. But the gravity on other planets is *very* different. Mars has a lot less gravity. So if you weighed 100 pounds on Earth, you'd weigh only 38 pounds there. But Jupiter's gravity has a much stronger pull—so you'd weigh 236 pounds there!

Just as God keeps us physically grounded with gravity, He keeps our hearts and minds grounded with His Word. It's full of all the wisdom and knowledge and encouragement and teaching we need. Read His Word every day. God's Word anchors us to truth, lifts us up to Him, and gives us an unchanging place to ground our lives. It's a force more powerful than any planet's gravity!

Dear Lord, teach me Your ways and show me how to live. Guide me with the truth of Your Word, and please forgive me when I do wrong.

BE AMAZED

Even though gravity has been around since God created the universe, Sir Isaac Newton first discovered it about 300 years ago. Legend says Newton was sitting under an apple tree when an apple fell on his head. In reality, he probably just saw the apple fall—and realized some sort of invisible force had made it fall. He called it *gravity*.

48

NO STANDING ON SATURN

Be on your guard; stand firm in the faith; be courageous; be strong.
—I CORINTHIANS 16:13 NIV

Saturn is often called the "Jewel of the Solar System" because of its beautiful rings. But this faraway planet is nothing like the Earth. It's the second-largest planet in our solar system (Jupiter is the biggest), and it has a small rocky core covered with gases. You couldn't even stand up on this ringed planet. In fact, because it's mostly made of gases, if you were to put Saturn in water—and you'd need a lot of water—it would float.

Another reason you couldn't stand up on Saturn is because it's an incredibly windy place. Winds around its equator, or middle, can reach up to 1,118 miles an hour. To understand just how fast that is, the fastest winds on Earth "only" get up to about 250 miles an hour—and they destroy *everything* in their path.

BE AMAZED

Saturn's glittering rings look pretty solid, but they aren't. They're made up of bits of dust, rock, and ice crystals—some as big as skyscrapers and others no bigger than a grain of sand. The biggest ring is so wide it could stretch more than 12 times the distance from the Earth to the Moon.

Sometimes it feels like you can't stand up even here on Earth. Troubles come roaring at you like 250-mile-an-hour winds—seeming as terribly powerful as a hurricane or tornado. Maybe a difficult problem is bothering you, a friend has betrayed you, a bully is picking on you, or people are pressuring you to do things you know are wrong. Or maybe someone else needs you to stand up for them. Whatever it is, you feel beat up and knocked around and even a little scared! But don't give up! You may not be able to stand up tall on Saturn, but you can stand up tall to any trouble because God is on your side. Pray hard, and hold on to Him. Not only will God protect you, but He'll also help you keep standing up for Him and for what's right until the storm of trouble is over.

Lord, sometimes my life feels like a windstorm is ripping through it. Please give me Your courage and strength so I can stand up tall and strong for You.

49

WHO'S THERE?

God did not give us a spirit that makes us afraid. He gave us a spirit of power and love and self-control.
—2 TIMOTHY 1:7

Have you ever thought your parents or teachers had eyes in the back of their heads? How do they see so much? While no person really has eyes in the back of her head, the owl butterfly does! Well, it has eyes on the back of its wings. Technically, they aren't really eyes—they're spots that *look* like eyes. You see, God gave the owl butterfly an amazing way to stay safe. The back of its wings look like the eyes of an owl. So when a predator zooms nearby looking for a tasty snack, it sees those "eyes" and thinks the butterfly is actually an owl. And since an owl just might turn that predator into a tasty snack, the predator quickly zooms away to search for less-threatening prey. God gave the owl butterfly a unique way to chase away its fear—its fear of being eaten, that is.

When you decide to follow God, He chases away your fears too. In fact, there are some things you'll *never* have to be frightened of again. Things like being alone—because God will never leave you (Deuteronomy 31:6). You don't have to fear mistakes either

BE AMAZED

God gave another type of butterfly an amazing way to hide from would-be predators. The wings of the leaf butterfly come in all sorts of brilliant colors when they're spread out flat. But when these butterflies fold up their wings, they look just like leaves. Some look like new green leaves, but others look like old, fallen brown leaves, allowing them to blend right in with their natural habitats!

---

because He'll always help you and forgive you when you ask (1 John 1:9). And, best of all, you'll never have to worry that God will stop loving you (Psalm 100:5). Because He won't. Not ever. Not for a single nanosecond, which is a billionth of a second, by the way. So the next time you're feeling a little frightened, remember who you are—a child of God—and let God chase away your fears!

Lord, sometimes I get scared—by the stuff happening around me, by the news, or just by worries of my own. When I do, remind me that You're always with me and always on my side.

50

CAN'T BE COUNTED

How precious are your thoughts about me, O God. They cannot be numbered! I can't even count them; they outnumber the grains of sand!
—PSALM 139:17–18 NLT

We like to count things. We count money. We count minutes. We count points—and a million other things. But some things we just cannot count.

We cannot count the number of stars in the universe—we don't even know how big the universe is! In our own Milky Way Galaxy, scientists believe

BE AMAZED

What's the biggest number known to man? Some people think it's the *googolplex*, which is a 1 followed by a *googol* of zeroes. (A googol is a 1 followed by 100 zeroes.) But the truth is, there is no biggest number. Why? Because you can always add one more.

there are as many as 400 billion stars, but they aren't sure. Why? Because they can't count them all!

Another thing that can't be counted are all the grains of sand on the Earth. Researchers estimate there are 7.5 quintillion grains of sand on the Earth's beaches. (That's 7,500,000,000,000,000,000!) Of course, that doesn't include all the other sand on the Earth—like the sand under the ocean.

But the most wonderful and amazing thing you cannot count is the number of thoughts God has about you. The God who created all those uncountable things—like stars and grains of sand—spends a whole lot of time thinking about . . . you. When you lie down to sleep, when you wake up in the morning, and every moment in between, God thinks about you. How indescribably awesome is that?

Lord, how wonderful it is to know that You think of me—and not just a little bit but too many times to be counted. I pray, God, that You will fill my mind with uncountable thoughts of You.

51

ATOMS, ELECTRONS, QUARKS, AND STUFF

**All things were made through him.
Nothing was made without him.**

—JOHN 1:3

An atom is the basic building block of all matter, of all things. And it's tiny—*really tiny*. In fact, 125 million atoms could fit inside a period. (Like the one at the end of that sentence . . . well . . . this one too.) Just one cell of your body contains about 100 trillion atoms. That's *100,000,000,000,000*! And your body contains roughly 37.2 trillion cells. So if you multiplied 100 trillion by 37.2 trillion . . . let's just say your body has *a whole lot* of atoms in it!

But things get smaller still because atoms are made up of even tinier things called *protons*, *neutrons*, and *electrons*. And those are made up of even tinier things called *quarks* and *leptons*. Someday we'll probably find out that quarks and leptons are made up of still tinier things!

All of these tiny particles come together to make everything you see—from each blade of grass to the tallest mountain to the faraway stars. Why does all this matter? Because God—who is Lord and Creator of all the hugeness of the universe—is also Lord and Creator of the tiniest of things. There's nothing too big or too small to be out of God's control.

For you, that means nothing is too big or too small to bring to God in prayer. No problem is so big He can't handle it. And no worry is so small He doesn't want to hear about it. Tell Him everything—good and bad, big and small, happy and sad—and then let Him take control.

Lord, thank You for always listening to me—about the big stuff, the little stuff, and all the other stuff in between. I know I can always talk to You and that You'll always answer. Thank You for taking care of all the details—the big ones and the tiny ones!

BE AMAZED

Elements form when a bunch of the same kinds of atoms join together. Long ago, people believed there were only 4 elements—air, water, fire, and earth. Now we know more than 100 elements exist, including metals like gold and silver and gases like hydrogen and oxygen. Also, 6 different elements make up 99 percent of your body: carbon, hydrogen, nitrogen, oxygen, phosphorus, and calcium.

52

NOT JUST ANOTHER SNOWFLAKE IN THE CROWD

You are the God who sees me.

—GENESIS 16:13 NIV

Snowflakes—so beautiful, so soft, and . . . so icy cold! One snowflake is a tiny, delicate thing, easily melted by the touch of your finger. But put a bunch of them together and they can blanket the world in shimmering white—or come crashing down a mountain in an avalanche that destroys everything in its path!

A snowflake forms high up in the clouds when a tiny water droplet freezes into an ice crystal. Water vapors in the cloud attach to the frozen crystal and stretch the snowflake into amazingly complex and creative shapes. Though the basic shape of a snowflake is almost always a hexagon (a shape with six sides), each snowflake becomes its own unique creation. Though it's hard to tell when they're all jumbled together in a big pile—or stuck together in a snowman—no two snowflakes are exactly the same. God created them each to be unique. Wow!

Do you ever feel like you're just another person in the crowd? That there's nothing special about you? If you've ever thought that—you're wrong. People have certain things in common—just as most all snowflakes are hexagons. But other things about you are just . . . *you*. God created you uniquely. You're never just another snowflake (person) in the crowd. *God sees you*. He sees when you're frightened and when you're lonely. He sees what you need, and He sees your hopes and dreams. God sees you and loves you and understands you. You're always somebody special to God.

BE AMAZED

No one else is like you on the planet—not now or ever. Just check out your fingerprints; even identical twins don't have the same ones. And that's not all that's unique about you. Scientists can now use the retinas of your eyes, the shape of your ears, and even your tongue print to identify you because no one else's are like yours!

Lord, when I feel like I'm nobody special, remind me that I'm always special to You. You know me inside and out, and You created me for a unique and special purpose.

53

LIGHT IT UP

"Let your light shine before others, that they may see your good deeds and glorify your Father in heaven."
—MATTHEW 5:16 NIV

Nothing says summertime like catching flashing fireflies on a warm night! You might know them by their other name: lightning bugs. Did you know these flashing creatures are actually beetles—and that more than 2,000

different species of them exist? They usually shine in colors of yellow, green, or orange. And each of those 2,000 species has its own pattern of flashing—it helps members of the same species recognize each other.

Fireflies are just one of many creatures that are *bioluminescent*, which is a gigantic word that simply means they make their own light. It's a chemical reaction inside the firefly that makes the light. That's the *how*, but *why?* Why do fireflies shine? Well, the guy fireflies do the shining, and they do it to catch the attention of the lady fireflies—who are attracted to all that light.

Something about things that light up the darkness makes you want to get a closer look. That's why Jesus tells you to let *your* light shine. Of course, your light doesn't shine because of a chemical reaction—it comes from God's Holy Spirit inside you. When you do things out of love—tough things like being kind to an enemy or forgiving someone who's hurt you—people see the light of Jesus shining out of you. That light shines just like a firefly shines in the dark, and people can't help but to come closer to check it out, which means you get to tell them about God. So get out there and shine your light!

BE AMAZED

A firefly's light is the most energy-efficient light in the world. That's because almost 100 percent of the energy from the chemical reaction becomes light. Compare that to an old-fashioned incandescent lightbulb, which releases only 10 percent of its energy as light and 90 percent as heat.

Lord, fill me so full with Your love that it shines out of me. Teach me to light up this world with everything I say and do.

54

PERFECTLY PLANNED AND CREATED

Lord, you are our father. We are like clay, and you are the potter. Your hands made us all.
—ISAIAH 64:8

There are some pretty interesting—really weird—animals in God's creation. One of them is the camel. With its thick, bushy eyebrows, long eyelashes, hump on its back, and big, floppy feet, the camel is not exactly the world's cutest creature. But everything about it was perfectly planned and created by God to help the camel live in the desert.

That big hump? Most people think it stores water, but it actually stores fat. That big hump of fat lets the camel go up to a week without drinking water during the summer and can go one or two weeks without eating. You know how? The camel can burn the fat in its hump for both energy and water. So what about those bushy eyebrows and long eyelashes? They keep out the desert sand. Camels can even close their nostrils to keep out the sand. And those big, floppy feet? They're perfect for traveling long distances on shifting sands.

Yes, camels were perfectly planned and created to live in the desert. Just as fish were perfectly created to live in water, birds were perfectly created to fly, and monkeys were perfectly created to swing through the trees. And *you* were perfectly created to be . . . you. Just as a potter shapes the clay into the vessel she wants to make, God made you *with* a plan and *for* a purpose—to love Him and to love others. And He gave you special talents and abilities so you could live out His purpose for you—in a uniquely *you* kind of way that no one else can do. God is the perfect Creator, and He created you according to His perfect plan!

BE AMAZED

Baby camels are born without any humps at all. Camels with one hump are called Arabian (or dromedary) camels. They live in the Middle East. Camels with two humps are called Asian (or Bactrian) camels. They live only in China and Mongolia.

Lord, I know I am Your creation, and You designed me just the way You wanted me to be. Please show me the talents You've given me, and help me use them in ways that make You smile and help others see You.

55

A STAR IS BORN

You created my inmost being; you knit me together in my mother's womb. I praise you because I am fearfully and wonderfully made; your works are wonderful, I know that full well.

—PSALM 139:13–14 NIV

The Whirlpool Galaxy is called a grand-design galaxy, and it is made up of hundreds of billions of stars, maybe as many as 500 billion! It's an incredibly beautiful spot in the universe, and it's also a very special one. That's because the Whirlpool Galaxy is a place where stars are born—a sort of baby hospital for stars. You see, in the beginning, God created the first stars in an instant when He said, "Let there be light!" Since then stars have formed when giant clouds of space dust and gases pull tighter and tighter and tighter together until . . . a star is born. As each star is born, God names it and carefully places it right where He wants it to be in His universe (Psalm 147:4). Wow!

BE AMAZED

Scientists say a star is born every 0.0002 seconds. Some of those stars are smaller, but some are as big as the Sun or even bigger.

The way God makes the stars *is* incredible, but what's even more incredible is the way He made you. He knit you together, one tiny cell at a time, in just the right way. Every part of you is exactly the way He wants you to be. God didn't just pay attention to the outside. He also carefully crafted talents and gifts and abilities and tucked them inside you—things no one else can do quite the same way you can.

You are God's *grandest* design—fearfully and wonderfully made by the Master Creator Himself! So if you ever find yourself thinking that you aren't special, that you don't have any talents, or something about you just isn't good enough, remember *who* made you, and then thank Him for His grand and awesome design. God made you, and He makes no mistakes.

God, thank You for making me just as I am. Help me use the talents and the abilities You've given me to tell everyone about how great You are.

56

ALL IN THE FAMILY

Be kind and loving to each other. Forgive each other just as God forgave you in Christ.

—EPHESIANS 4:32

"He hit me!" "She took my stuff!" "I had it first!" Do you have brothers or sisters? If you do, have they ever said anything like that? Have you? That's what people call *sibling rivalry,* and it's a fancy way to describe not getting along with your brothers and sisters. But people aren't the only ones with this problem—animal brothers and sisters have it too.

Just think of those poor naked mole rats—they can have hundreds of siblings, all from the same mother! And older naked mole rats aren't shy about forcing younger ones to move out of the way in their underground tunnel systems. And then there's the cattle egret, which takes sibling rivalry to a deadly level. When one chick gets stronger than the other, it actually kills its sibling and throws it out of the nest while the parents are out hunting for food. *Yikes!*

Fortunately, most animal siblings get along much better than that. For example, older elephant "children" babysit younger ones. Otter pups spend almost all their time together and will even hold hands in the water so they don't float apart! And lion sisters stay together for life in a group called a pride.

Here's the thing: when you live with someone all the time—like a brother or sister—it's easy to get on each other's nerves. (*You* might even get on their nerves!) Then the next thing you know, you're arguing, fussing, and fighting. Ask God to help you love your family, to be kind, to be patient, and to forgive each other when you make mistakes. After all, that's what God does for you!

Lord, You know that sometimes it's hard for me to get along with my family, especially my brothers and sisters. Help me to be kind—especially when I don't really want to be.

BE AMAZED

The European shrew is so tiny that a whole litter of babies can fit inside a teaspoon. But these tiny guys really stick together. When they have to move because danger is coming, they travel in a sort of "shrew caravan." Mom leads the way with the kiddos following behind—each holding the tail of the sibling in front of it between its teeth.

RUMBLE, GRUMBLE, GROWL

Do everything without grumbling or arguing.
—PHILIPPIANS 2:14 NIV

It always seems to happen at the worst possible times—in the middle of a test or in the middle of a prayer. Whenever everything is still and quiet, that's when it strikes: the dreaded, loud gurgling of your stomach. What does it mean? And why does it happen?

Stomach growling starts—you guessed it—in your stomach. Then it moves to your small intestine and the rest of your digestive system. You see, when you eat, your body squeezes its muscles to push the food through your digestive system. Add to that some liquids and some digestive juices, and it all turns into a gooey mess called *chyme*. The grumbling comes when air and gases get added to the chyme. When those gases get squeezed by the muscles in your stomach, the result is *rumble, grumble, growl*. Those rumbles can happen at any time, but when not much food is in there, the grumbling can really get loud. Think of it as your body's way of reminding you to eat.

BE AMAZED

Did you know there's a name for those rumbling noises your tummy makes? It's *borborygmi*. That word is an example of *onomatopoeia*, which is a word that sounds like what it means. Try saying *borborygmi* (bor-bo-rig-my). Doesn't it sort of sound like a tummy rumbling? Other onomatopoeic words are *swish, whoosh, splash, murmur*, and *plop*.

Another part of your body can grumble too, and that's your mouth. When you've got homework or chores to do, or when you're asked to do something you just don't want to do—do you ever grumble? Do you ever argue or complain? God sure hopes you don't. If you find your lips making noises they shouldn't, stop. You're probably going to have to do that chore anyway, so you might as well try smiling about it. When you need to do something you don't want to do, remember all the amazing things God does for you every day, and tell Him "thank You" instead of complaining. You'll find that giving Him praise will make you feel a lot better than grumbling to yourself. And you'll be making God smile too.

God, I know sometimes I argue and complain. Help me to hear myself rumbling and grumbling—and to choose to worship You instead.

58

THE PLANNER

"I know what I have planned for you," says the Lord. "I have good plans for you. I don't plan to hurt you. I plan to give you hope and a good future."

—JEREMIAH 29:11

BE AMAZED

The Hubble Space Telescope is so powerful that it can see stars, planets, and galaxies so far away that it would be as if you were able to see a lightning bug way over in Japan while sitting in your home in the United States.

For centuries, scientists and astronomers have been trying to discover the secrets of the universe—how it began, how it works, and our place in it. Scientists built the Hubble Space Telescope to discover some of those secrets. Launched in 1990, it's the first major telescope to be placed in space. Traveling far above Earth's clouds and atmosphere, it has a clear view of the universe. It has photographed the planets of our solar system as well as faraway stars and galaxies. Hubble's photographs have changed how we see the universe and our place in it, and it has helped us recognize that our universe was no accident.

God isn't about chaos or accidents or messes. Our God is a planner. He designed everything in His universe to work together perfectly. The Sun is just the right distance from Earth. The Moon's gravity is perfect for our ocean's tides. The Earth tilts just perfectly to keep our climate balanced. Everything in the universe works together because that's how God planned it.

And do you know what else God planned? Your life. All the days of your life were planned out and written in God's book—before you were even born (Psalm 139:16). And God's plans for you are good ones. Yes, there'll still be bad days, but God even has a plan for the tough times. He'll use them to make you more like Him. God is the ultimate planner—and He has amazing plans for you!

Lord, this universe that You planned and created is indescribably amazing. But what I love most is that You love me—teeny, tiny me—so much that You have good and perfect plans for me.

59

UNLIKELY FRIENDS

"God does not see the same way people see. People look at the outside of a person, but the Lord looks at the heart."
—1 SAMUEL 16:7

How would *you* like to hang out with a shark? Not me, but thanks for asking. Yet one fish actually hangs out with a shark—*all* the time. It's called the remora fish. Its head is like a big, flat suction cup. It suctions itself right to the shark, hanging on for the ride wherever the shark goes. When the shark eats a meal, the remora lets go and munches on the leftovers. *Yummy.* Sometimes it cleans the shark's body—including the shark's *mouth*—to get rid of any parasites or food stuck in the shark's teeth. Then the remora suctions itself back on for the next ride. The shark gets cleaned and the remora gets fed. It's a win-win for this pair of unlikely friends.

Who would have thought that a shark and a fish could be friends? It just proves that you really can't judge a book by its cover—or a friend by how he or she looks on the outside. You've probably noticed that the world likes to judge people by their skin color, their clothes, their hair, where they're from, how much money they have, or how they talk. But God says those things don't matter—not to Him. And they shouldn't matter to you either. Instead, you should look at a person's heart. Is he kind? Is she helpful? Does this person love God? That's what is really important. And when you start looking at the inside of a person, instead of the outside, you just might find yourself in an unlikely—but wonderful—friendship. (I'd still stay away from sharks, though!)

Lord, help me not to judge people based on what they look like on the outside. Help me instead to look at the heart—just as You do.

BE AMAZED

Caterpillars and ants are another pair of unlikely friends. The caterpillars produce a kind of sugar on their skin for the ants to eat. In turn, the ants protect the caterpillars from predators like wasps and assassin bugs. The ants get food, and the caterpillars get protection—a win-win for these bug besties.

60

BIG KIDS DO CRY

Jesus wept.

—JOHN 11:35 NIV

Crying. It starts the moment you're born—literally. And it just keeps happening, no matter how old you are. It can happen when you're sad or frightened, when you're happy—or even when you're outside on a windy day or inside chopping up an onion. So what's up with all these tears?

Did you know there are actually three different types of tears? *Continuous* (or basal) tears are the ones you have all the time. They keep your eyes moist and seeing clearly. Then there are *reflex* tears. They happen on windy days and when you're cutting onions. But it's the third type that you usually think of—*psychogenic* tears. Those are the tears you cry when you're sad, afraid, or overjoyed.

When tears run down your face, do you ever wonder what God does while you're hurting? Well, the Bible says exactly what He does. God sees your tears, keeps a list of them, and then tucks them safely into a bottle to keep (Psalm 56:8). That's proof of just how much He cares for you.

BE AMAZED

Why does your nose always seem to get drippy and sniffly when you're crying? Well, it's because tears—at least the ones that don't run down your face—actually drain into your nasal cavity through tiny holes in the inside corners of your eyelids. Once there, either you swallow the tears—or they drip out your nose. And you thought only your eyes cried!

God doesn't stop with just *seeing* your tears. He weeps right along with you. Jesus showed this when His friend Lazarus died. Lazarus's sisters, Mary and Martha, were crying, and the Bible says Jesus wept too. Now Jesus knew He was about to raise Lazarus from the dead and this story would have a happy ending. So why did He cry? Because His friends were hurting. And, since Jesus is your friend, He hurts and weeps with you when you're hurting—even while He knows exactly what He's going to do to give your story a glorious ending.

Lord, thank You for always being right by my side, especially when I'm hurting. It comforts me to know that You feel my pain—and that You work to make things right.

61

ALL TWISTED UP

"Be still and know that I am God."
—PSALM 46:10

The tornado, or "twister," is one of the most fascinating—and terrifying—of storms. These violently spinning tubes of air stretch from the clouds all the way down to the ground. Most tornadoes have wind speeds of less than a hundred miles per hour, but some can reach more than *300 miles per hour*!

Have you ever seen a tornado? They start out almost clear, like the air they're made of. But as they spin, they pick up bits of dust and mud and wreckage, which give them their eerie, dark colors. A tornado might touch down on the ground for only a few seconds and travel a few hundred feet, or it may last longer than an hour and travel for miles. The faster its wind and the longer it stays on the ground, the more damage a tornado can cause. Weak tornadoes may only knock off a tree limb or two, but strong ones can completely rip a house off its foundation and send cars hurtling through the air like missiles.

Sometimes, troubles can be kind of like tornadoes. A small one can wreck a day, but a big one can leave you feeling all twisted up inside for a while. What should you do when everything is spinning out of control? *Stop.* That's right. Just stop. "Be still," says the Lord, "and know that I am God." Remind yourself that God is bigger than any trouble, and He'll never leave you to face a storm alone. He has the power to stop even the strongest tornado.

BE AMAZED

Tornadoes hit the United States more than any other country in the world—more than 1,200 each year. Most occur in "Tornado Alley," which is in the Midwest. Texas has the most tornadoes each year. It gets about 155, Kansas has about 96, Florida gets about 66, and Oklahoma has about 62.

Lord, when the troubles of this world swirl around me like the winds of a tornado, please help me remember that You are bigger and stronger. I trust You to keep me safe during life's storms.

62

WHEN YOU'VE BEEN ECLIPSED

Be happy with those who are happy.
Be sad with those who are sad.
—ROMANS 12:15

Your best friend made the team, but you didn't. Your sister made straight As, but you didn't. Should you pout or sulk or just not speak to them anymore? Or maybe *you* made the team, but now your friend is upset. And perhaps *you* got the As, while your sister didn't do so well. What should you do?

When one person seems to outshine another, it's kind of like this thing that happens to our Sun and Moon called an *eclipse*.

An eclipse occurs when a planet or a moon passes between two astronomical objects, such as another planet, moon, or the Sun. When the Moon lines up between the Sun and the Earth, the Moon blocks the Sun's light. That's called a *solar eclipse*. When the Earth gets between the Sun and Moon, it blocks the Sun's light to the Moon. That's called a *lunar eclipse*. A lunar eclipse can last as long as a few hours, while a solar eclipse lasts only a few minutes.

So sometimes it's the Sun's turn to shine, and sometimes it's the Moon's turn to reflect the Sun's light. It's the same with people. Sometimes it's your turn to shine—to be the winner, make the team, or ace the test. And sometimes it's your turn to be "eclipsed," while someone else shines. What do you do? God says, "Be happy with those who are happy. Be sad with those who are sad." If your friend is celebrating, celebrate too—even if things didn't turn out so great for you. And if your friend is sad, that's not the time to brag. Be humble, and offer comfort and encouragement instead—because that's what good friends do.

Lord, it's tough when things don't happen the way I want. But help me to be happy for my friends when they succeed and to be humble when it's my turn to win.

Solar Eclipse

Lunar Eclipse

BE AMAZED

Long ago, people thought that the Earth was flat and that you could actually sail right off the edge! But lunar eclipses helped them discover the Earth is round. That's because during a lunar eclipse, the Earth's shadow can be seen on the face of the Moon. When people saw the shadow was round, they figured out the Earth must be too!

63

LOOK OUT! IT'S GONNA BLOW!

People with understanding control their anger;
a hot temper shows great foolishness.
—PROVERBS 14:29 NLT

Imagine an explosion so powerful that it shoots molten rock and ash hundreds of feet into the air, triggering massive fires, tsunamis, and electrical storms. Sounds like something out of a science-fiction movie, doesn't it? But it's not fiction; it's science! The science of an erupting volcano, that is.

Some 1,500 active volcanoes are on the Earth, and about 20 of them are actively erupting right this second! So how do volcanoes erupt? Well, remember the outermost layer of the Earth is called the crust. And the Earth's crust isn't completely solid. It's made up of giant puzzle pieces called *tectonic plates*. Under those plates (about 18 miles or so below the Earth's surface) is a layer of hot liquid rock called *magma*, along with a bunch of explosive gases. As the tectonic plates "float" atop the magma, they rub against each other. At the same time, pressure builds up in the magma and gases until . . . *ka-boom*! This molten hot mixture explodes up through cracks in the Earth's crust. The magma, which is called *lava* when it passes Earth's surface, spews out at temperatures of more than 2,000 degrees Fahrenheit, scorching and burning anything it touches.

BE AMAZED

The largest above-ground volcano in the world, which is more than 2.5 miles high, is Mauna Loa in Hawaii. But there's an even bigger volcano—on Mars! That's right. The tallest volcano in our solar system is Mars' Olympus Mons. This volcano is 13 miles high and 373 miles wide.

Does that image of an erupting volcano remind you of anything or *anyone*? Words like *hot* and *explosive* not only describe volcanoes, they can also describe your temper. Of course, everyone gets angry—even Jesus did. But how you handle your anger makes all the difference. If you find yourself starting to "spew" angry words or "explode" at whoever gets in your path, take a deep breath and get out of there. Get away by yourself and talk to God. Tell Him what's going on, and ask Him to show you how to handle your anger the right way. Because you don't want people saying, "Look out! He's (or she's) gonna blow!" about you.

Lord, when I get angry, help me not to spew foolish and angry words that only make things worse. Instead, give me the words and the wisdom to make things better.

64

SO BIG!

And these are only a small part of God's works. We only hear a small whisper of him. So who can understand God's thundering power?

—JOB 26:14

Some stars are huge—I mean blow-your-mind huge! There's one star that scientists call VY Canis Majoris, which is 1.7 billion miles wide. If Earth were the size of a golf ball, VY Canis Majoris would be the height of Mount Everest, which is 29,029 feet tall.

Stars are also powerful. The Eta Carinae star system is one of the brightest in our galaxy. It's 90 times bigger than our Sun and 5 million times brighter! But even that's not the brightest. Dying stars can shine even brighter. At one point during its death, the Supernova 1987A shone as brightly as *100 million* of our Suns.

And our God made them all—and zillions more. That's how big and how mighty and how powerful our God is. So there is nothing in your life He can't handle. Got a bully bugging you? Ask God to help. Having trouble being kind to your brother or sister? Ask God to help. Is something else troubling you? You guessed it—ask God to help. The One who made the stars will be right there with you.

Sometimes God will make the problem simply go away. Or He may send someone your way to help you. Or He'll remind you of His Word. But God will always walk with you through the trouble, giving you His strength and His power to do the right thing, even when it's hard. There's no problem too big or too little for God to help you handle. It's just like the song says: *Our God is so big, so strong and so mighty. There's nothing our God cannot do!*

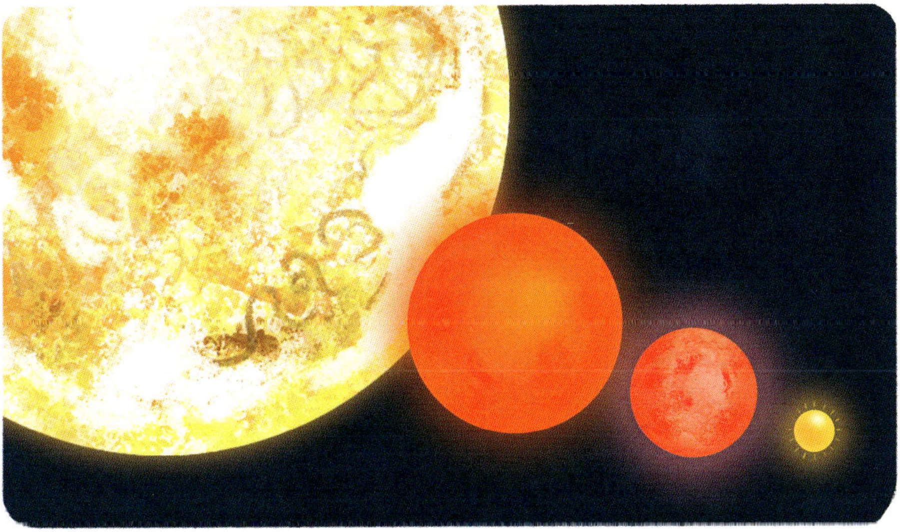

God, I know there's nothing You cannot do, so I trust You to help me handle anything that comes my way today.

BE AMAZED

So far, the record for the biggest star in the universe goes to UY Scuti. It's a bright-red supergiant located 9,500 light-years away. Scientists believe it's 1,700 times bigger than our Sun. But scientists continue to discover new stars all the time, so only God knows if UY Scuti really is the biggest star in the universe.

65

DINOSAUR ROCK

"Love each other. You must love each other as I have loved you. All people will know that you are my followers if you love each other."
—JOHN 13:34–35

Not all rocks are just rocks. Some are actually fossils—rocks with the imprints of ancient animals or plants left in them. You see, when an animal dies, its body quickly decays and disappears most of the time. But if an animal dies in a watery area, its body might sink into mud, or be quickly covered with

muddy soil. When this happens, the soft parts of the animal's body—like its skin or internal organs—decompose, but the hard parts—like teeth and bones—are preserved. Over a long period of time, sedimentary rocks form around these animal remains, thereby forming fossils. (*Sedimentary* rocks form when small bits of rocks, shells, or bones cement together.) Plants, animal footprints, burrows, and even poop can all become fossils!

BE AMAZED

Imagine an animal about the size of a squirrel with a big, soft, bushy tail. Now imagine it with big eyes and a longer snout—and fangs! That's exactly what scientists think they've found in some fossils collected in Argentina, and they're calling this extinct creature the saber-toothed squirrel.

Scientists called *paleontologists* study fossils and are able to learn a lot about ancient plants and animals by studying what they've left behind in the rocks. Without fossils, we wouldn't even know dinosaurs existed!

Did you know that you also leave fossils—or at least impressions—behind wherever you go? Okay, so they're not really rocks. Instead, you leave impressions on people's hearts by what you do and say, and the way you make people feel. Jesus said you'd be able to tell which people belong to Him by the love and kindness they show to others. So do you make people feel good when they're around you? Or do they run from you as if you were a Tyrannosaurus rex? Just as scientists learn about dinosaurs from the fossil impressions they leave behind, people learn about Jesus from the impressions His people leave behind. Make sure your "fossils" are ones the Rock—that's Jesus—would be proud of!

Lord, teach me to love others as You have loved me. Let the "fossil impressions" I leave behind be ones that make people want to learn more about You.

66

WE'RE ALL IN THIS TOGETHER

The human body has many parts, but the many parts make up one whole body. So it is with the body of Christ. . . . God has put each part just where he wants it.
—1 CORINTHIANS 12:12, 18 NLT

Your body is made up of trillions of cells—which are the basic building blocks of all life. Remember, scientists think your body has somewhere around 37.2 trillion cells! And every cell has a job. Some cells work to build up skin and bones, others produce energy, some carry oxygen, others do your thinking, some sense what's happening around you, others attack germs—the list goes on and on. So, basically, your entire body is like an electric company, transportation center, communications network, hospital, and battlefield all rolled into one. That's the way God created your body—with all those cells working together to do amazing stuff!

Here's the thing: your cells have to work *together* or your body won't work. Imagine if a heart cell said, "I don't feel like pumping anymore." Or a nerve cell said, "I'm just not feeling it today." God created your cells to work *together*.

That's also the way God created His body of followers—to work together. Just like a cell, each person has a job. Some Christians teach and preach, others lead singing, some are artists or writers, some are great at math, and others feed the poor, help the sick, and take out the trash from the church building. It's easy to think that some jobs are better or even "godlier" than others. But that's

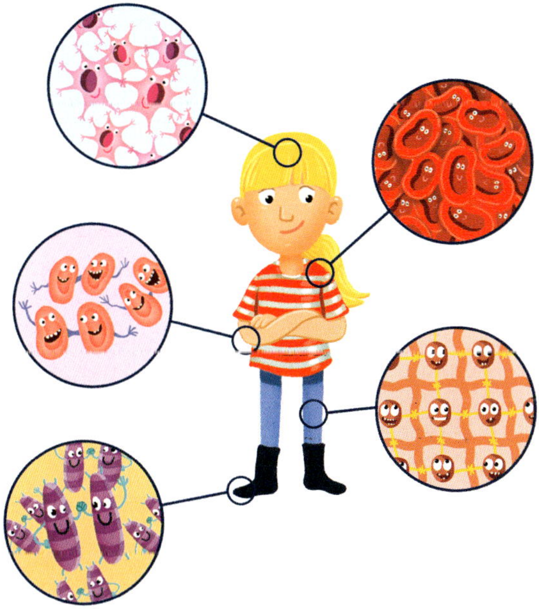

not true! *Every* job is important. And all of us "cells" have to work together so the "body" of Christ can do what it needs to do—be His helpers on Earth.

Dear God, I understand that I'm a "cell" in the body of Your kingdom. Show me what job you need me to do—and help me to do it the very best that I can!

BE AMAZED

Your body actually has more bacteria cells than human cells. *Gross!* But bacteria cells are so small that if you collected all the bacteria in your body, it would only fill up a half-gallon milk jug. Bacteria helps your body digest foods and fight off illness. So as it turns out, all that "grossness" is really pretty good for you.

67

IT'S A REAL GEM!

We have this treasure from God. But we are only like clay jars that hold the treasure. This shows that this great power is from God, not from us.
—2 CORINTHIANS 4:7

Twinkle, twinkle little . . . *planet?* That's right. Scientists have discovered a planet—55 Cancri E—that is thought to be covered in diamonds and graphite (unlike the Earth's surface, which is covered in water and granite). In fact, scientists estimate that at least one-third of this planet's mass could be made of diamonds. That's enough for a lot of diamond rings!

Discovered in 2004, 55 Cancri E is 40 light-years away from the Earth—that's 40 multiplied by 5.88 trillion miles! The diamond planet orbits at a super-fast speed around its own sun. Its year, or one full orbit around its sun, lasts just 18 hours, while Earth's lasts 365 days.

Experts guess the planet's diamonds are worth $26.9 nonillion—that's 269 followed by 29 zeroes! That's more dollars than you'll ever have! But before you rush off to do a little treasure hunting on 55 Cancri E, you should know that not only is this planet farther away than you can travel, but it's also a bit warm . . . 4,400 degrees Fahrenheit.

BE AMAZED

Scientists have discovered several amazing—and, well, just plain weird—planets floating around in space. One of the strangest is the "Blue Marble" planet (also known by its more boring name of HD 189733b). It is 63 light-years away, and its temperatures soar to 1,700 degrees Fahrenheit. But what's weird is that its blue color comes from an atmosphere that rains molten glass—sideways—in winds faster than 4,000 miles per hour!

But you're in luck because there's an even greater treasure—and it's much closer to home. It's the treasure of God's Holy Spirit. In fact, when you became a follower of Christ, this treasure came to live right inside you. He's your Helper, your Comforter, and your Guide. He "[teaches] you everything" and helps "you to remember all the things" Jesus spoke in His Word (John 14:26). He's the Spirit of God *living* inside you! And that's a treasure worth more than a whole planet full of diamonds.

Lord, thank You for the treasure of the Holy Spirit that You've hidden inside me. Help me listen to His voice, so I can learn more about how to live for You.

68

THE SCOOP ON SKIN

He will cover you with his feathers, and under his wings you can hide. His truth will be your shield and protection.
—PSALM 91:4 NCV

There's a lot more to your skin than meets the eye. First of all, your skin is actually an organ—just like your heart, lungs, and kidneys. In fact, it's the largest organ of your entire body. The average-sized person has 22 square feet of skin! That's about the size of a small blanket. Skin comes in all different colors—all created by God using a pigment called *melanin*. Think of melanin like an artist would think about paint. The more melanin you have, the darker your skin. The less you have, the paler your skin.

Skin not only covers your bones and muscles, it also senses the environment around you and helps control your body's temperature. Your skin sweats to cool you off when you get hot, and it closes up its pores to keep in the heat (think of goose bumps!) when you're cold. But one of your skin's most important jobs is to protect the rest of your body from injury and disease. It's like a shield for your body.

And while your skin is the shield for your body, God is the shield for your heart, mind, spirit, *and* body. It's easy to be afraid and anxious about the bad things that could happen in the world. But the Bible is filled with God's promises to watch over and protect you, like this promise God gave in Psalm 18:30: "The Lord's words are pure. He is a shield to those who trust him." And this one: "He is our help, our shield to protect us" (Psalm 33:20). And: "The Lord is my strength and shield. I trust him, and he helps me" (Psalm 28:7). The list could go on and on. So when you're scared or feeling threatened, run to God, and He'll be your shield!

God, You are my rock, my protection, my Savior, and my shield. When times get tough, I'm so thankful You surround me and keep me safe.

BE AMAZED

Here are some weird skin facts: Underneath all its fur, a polar bear's skin is black. A rhinoceros's skin can be almost 2 inches thick. And frogs? Their skin is really unique. Instead of drinking water through their mouths, they actually soak it in through their skin!

69

ROCK SOLID

"The wise man built his house on rock. It rained hard and the water rose. The winds blew and hit that house. But the house did not fall, because the house was built on rock."
—MATTHEW 7:24–25

The next time you're outside, take a good, close look at the rocks around you. Have you ever wondered what they're actually made of? Well, that depends on what *kinds* of rock they are.

Rocks form in one of three different ways, and each of those ways has a specific name. The first are *igneous* rocks. They form when magma (remember, that's underground lava) cools and becomes solid. Granite and pumice are igneous rocks. *Sedimentary* rocks, like limestone and sandstone, are the second kind of rock. They form when bits of other rocks, shells, or bones collect and harden together, often at the bottoms of lakes and oceans. Finally, there are *metamorphic* rocks. These rocks form when other types of rocks are put under extreme pressure in blazing hot temperatures for long periods of time, causing them to

change or *metamorphisize*. They include marble (which comes from limestone) and quartzite (which comes from sandstone).

For centuries, people have used rocks for everything from weapons to tools to jewelry. But one of their most common uses is for building. Why? Because they're heavy and solid. They can't be blown down by just any old rain or wind. You can count on rocks!

Did you know God is sometimes called the Rock (Psalm 18:2)? No rocks on the Earth can even compare with His strength, but they do help you understand how much you can count on Him to protect and save you. His love for you is solid—it doesn't change, no matter what else in this world does. And when you build your life on Him, He won't let *any* storms blow you down.

Lord, You are my Rock. You protect me, You hold me up, and You are the solid foundation for my life. Thank You, God.

BE AMAZED

Some rocks are out of this world. No, really! They come from outer space. When a meteor hits the Earth's atmosphere, most of it burns away. But what's left—the part that hits the Earth—is called a *meteorite*. The biggest ever found was back in 1920. It's called the Hoba Meteorite. It's 9 feet long and 9 feet wide, and it weighs 66 tons.

70

THAT'S INCREDIBLE!

With God nothing will be impossible.

—LUKE 1:37 NKJV

The human body can be trained to do amazing—and seemingly impossible—things! For example, Olympian Usain Bolt ran the 100-meter race in just 9.58 seconds, and he is considered the fastest man alive. Florence Griffith Joyner—the world's fastest woman—ran that same 100 meters in just 10.49 seconds. Compare that speed to a cheetah, which can run 100 meters in 5.95 seconds. That's if a cheetah wanted to run a race, of course.

Other people have trained themselves to swim as fast as fish. Olympic swimmer Michael Phelps can swim 100 meters in just 51 seconds, and Katie Ledecky can swim it in just 53.75 seconds. Amazing!

Yes, humans can train their bodies to do incredible things. But when you combine the human body with the power of God, that's when things get truly incredible. Sometimes God gives His followers amazing strength—like Samson, who killed a lion and later tore down a temple, both with his bare hands. Other times, God gives His people the courage to do great things—like when Esther risked her life to go before King Xerxes to save her people. Or when David faced Goliath since no one else would. Or when Gideon took on an entire army with just 300 men. And sometimes God gives His people the words He wants them to say—just as He did for Moses, Peter, and Paul.

But God doesn't give miraculous strength just to people in the Bible. He gives the same supernatural help to you too. God gives you the strength to stand up to temptation. He gives you the courage to do what's right when everyone else is doing wrong. And He gives you the words to share His good news. Because with God, incredible—even impossible—things happen all the time!

BE AMAZED

The world's fastest bird is the peregrine falcon, which can reach speeds of up to 200 miles per hour in a dive. The fastest sea animal is the sailfish, with speeds up to 68 miles an hour. But the fastest land animal we know of was a cheetah named Sarah at the Cincinnati Zoo, with a record speed of 61 miles per hour.

Dear God, You created me in an amazing and wonderful way. Please use my body, mind, and spirit to tell others about You.

71

JUST THE RIGHT SIZE

Praise him, sun and moon. Praise him, all you shining stars. Praise him, highest heavens.
—PSALM 148:3–4

So just how big is the universe? Well . . . actually . . . we have no idea.

The Sun—our closest star—is 93 million miles away from the Earth. Our galaxy, the Milky Way, is so big that if you jumped in the very fastest spaceship ever made, it would take 100,000 light-years to travel across it. And our

nearest neighbor galaxy, the Canis Major Dwarf Galaxy? It's 25,000 light-years away. (Remember, a light-year is how far light can travel in a year, which is 5.88 trillion miles. So if you multiply that by 25,000—well, let's just say that's an incredible number!)

With the Hubble Space Telescope—a powerful telescope that orbits the Earth and takes pictures far beyond what we can see on our own—we have been able to see some incredible things, like galaxies as far as 12 billion light-years away. And that's just what we know about so far. It's called the "Known Universe." Scientists believe there's much more to discover. It's as if God is saying, *"Build a bigger telescope, and I'll show you some really amazing stuff. I've got stuff up here that will blow your mind!"*

But all of these discoveries have some scientists stumped. They wonder: *How could a universe this big be just for us?* And you know what? They're right . . . this universe is too big for just us. But what if God didn't just make the universe to be our home? What if God made the universe to show off the splendor and majesty and greatness and glory of who *He* is and how huge *He* is? Then the universe isn't too big at all. It's exactly the right size . . . it's God-size.

BE AMAZED

In 1924, Edwin Hubble was the first to prove that other galaxies exist far beyond the Milky Way Galaxy. (The Hubble Space Telescope was named after him!) Since then, the Hubble Space Telescope has discovered billions of galaxies—and scientists believe billions more exist that we haven't found yet.

God, You are so big and so powerful. Thank You for creating a universe so big that it reminds me of Your power. You are just the right size for me.

72

BRAIN POWER

Love the Lord your God. Love him with all your heart, all your soul, all your strength, and all your mind.

—LUKE 10:27

Your brain is a lot more than just a 3-pound blob of wrinkly, pinkish-gray jelly. Your brain is faster than the fastest computer. It controls your entire body—from your breathing to your heart beating to your sleeping—and everything in between. It tells you what you're seeing, smelling, tasting, hearing, and touching. Your brain not only does your thinking, it also stores your memories and imagines your dreams. It tells you when to laugh, when to cry, and what to do when you're angry. Scientists haven't even figured out what all your brain does, and they definitely don't understand *how* it does it all.

God understands, though. He created your brain—along with the rest of your body—and He says it is "fearfully and wonderfully made" (Psalm 139:14 NIV). But God didn't create your brain just to sit in your head like a lump. He wants you to use it for His glory. That means using your brain power to think of new ways to help others, to serve Him, and to tell others about Him. It means filling your mind with His Word by reading and memorizing the Scriptures. God made only one brain like yours, and He gave it to you!

When you're faced with a problem so big it's got you worried, use your brain to remind yourself of who God is and what He's promised to you—to never leave you, to love you forever, and to always protect you. Then, when the problem is solved, use your brain to praise God. Your brain is a gift from God—be sure to use it!

Dear God, fill my mind with thoughts of the wonders of You. And help me to use my brain power to think of new ways to serve You.

BE AMAZED

The sperm whale has the largest brain of any animal, with a brain that weighs 17 pounds and can grow up to 500 cubic inches in size. Compare that to the human brain, which weighs only about 3 pounds. But all that size doesn't make the whale smarter. Intelligence comes from how the brain works and how big it is compared to the rest of the body. And that's where humans are "heads above" the rest!

73

FOGGY DAZE

**God, examine me and know my heart.
Test me and know my thoughts.**
—PSALM 139:23

Fog . . . it's a must-have for any spooky movie or ghostly campfire tale. It creeps in low and damp and cool, adding a filmy layer of mystery to everything it covers. You may have seen it blocking your view outside, especially if you're awake early in the morning. So what *is* fog?

BE AMAZED

Not much rainfall is in the Atacama Desert, along the coast of Chile. But there is a *lot* of fog. The villagers there have figured out a way to capture the water in the fog using nets, so they can make drinking water. A clever solution to a thirsty problem!

Fog is actually a cloud flying low to the ground—a *stratus cloud,* to be exact, made up of a collection of tiny water droplets or ice crystals. These droplets are so tiny and so lightweight they float on the air.

Fogs usually live only a short time. As soon as the Sun rises, the heat from its rays "burns" away the fog (think of it like melting!) and makes everything clear again.

This is also exactly what happens with the Son (Jesus). You see, sometimes this world tells you lies—and they're easy to believe. Lies like: "You'll never be good for anything" or "Nobody cares about you." Or lies like: "You can't do anything right" or "You're worthless." Those kinds of thoughts can "fog" up your brain so you can't see the truth. When your thoughts get stuck in a foggy daze, that's when it's time to go soak in the Son. Talk to Jesus. Read about how much He loves you and how wonderfully He made you. His Word is always truthful and always gives light. And the Son's light will always burn away the "fog" of this world's lies.

Lord, it's so easy to get stuck in a fog of lies. Sometimes I can't see or think clearly because of them. Please "burn" away the fog and show me the truth of Your promises.

74

WHO'S HUNTING WHO?

Stay alert! Watch out for your great enemy, the devil. He prowls around like a roaring lion, looking for someone to devour.

—I PETER 5:8 NLT

Predators are animals that hunt and eat other animals. On the other hand, the animals that are hunted and eaten are called *prey*. When you think of predators, you probably think of roaring lions or snarling grizzly bears, but did you know that ladybugs are also predators? That's right: they eat other bugs. And that sweet little bird on your bird feeder? It doesn't eat just seeds. It also hunts down worms and other insects.

Just as predators come in all shapes and sizes, they also have different hunting methods. Some predators, like hawks, chase down their prey. Others, like wolves, stalk their prey by quietly sneaking up on it. Some predators, like alligators, ambush their prey, which means they hide and wait until prey wanders near enough to be snatched. To survive, it's important for prey animals to always stay alert.

It's important for you to stay alert too. That's because a predator is hunting you, and his name is Satan. The Bible says he prowls around like a roaring lion to stalk you! Satan uses the same hunting methods as animal predators. He'll try to chase you down and trap you in troubles. He'll stalk you with temptation, hoping you'll mess up and sin. He'll try to ambush you—waiting for you to let your guard down by not staying close to God. Watch out for traps, and stay close to God by talking to Him, praising Him, and studying His Word every single day. Don't be easy prey! God is more powerful than Satan, and He is always able to protect you from any of Satan's schemes.

Dear God, I pray You will open my eyes to see the devil's traps. And I pray You will give me the courage and strength to stay away from them. Thank You for leading me!

BE AMAZED

Different predators have different weapons to kill their prey. Bears have claws, sharks have teeth, and spiders have poison. But the chameleon has . . . its tongue. That's right. The chameleon's tongue—which can be more than 7 inches long—is covered in a sticky, glue-like substance. When the chameleon shoots its tongue out, the prey sticks to it and then gets slurped back into the chameleon's mouth.

75

IT'S UNIVERSAL

"I am putting my rainbow in the clouds. It is the sign of the agreement between me and the earth."
—GENESIS 9:13

The Earth isn't the only planet in our solar system with a moon. Saturn has one too. Well, actually it has 53 moons! One of them is called Titan. This faraway moon has something else you might have thought only the Earth had—rainbows.

Here on the Earth, rainbows happen when light from the Sun bounces in and out of water droplets in the air, especially after a rain shower. Titan's moon is wet, but not with water. Its moisture contains methane—a gas that is poisonous to humans. So Titan's rainbows form when the light bounces in and out of the droplets of methane. Deadly to humans, but beautiful!

Do you remember the story of the very first rainbow? It came after the Great Flood. The world had become so wicked that God caused a flood to destroy every living thing—except Noah, his family, and the animals on the ark. Noah was saved because he loved God. When Noah and his family stepped off the ark, God made them a promise: He would never again flood the entire Earth. Then God put a rainbow in the sky as a sign of His promise.

So why is a rainbow on a faraway moon called Titan important? Because it tells you something about God: His promises are universal! No matter what's happening, how old you are, or *where* you are—even on a moon called Titan—God keeps His promises. Every single one. Pretty awesome, huh?

God, You promise to love me forever and to always help me. I am so glad I know You'll keep every single one of those promises.

BE AMAZED

You've surely seen a rainbow before, and maybe even a double rainbow. But have you ever seen a *full-circle rainbow*? Probably not . . . unless you're an astronaut, an airline pilot, or you just happen to be standing at the top of Niagara Falls. That's because you need to be up above the water droplets to see a rainbow's full circle—otherwise, half of the circle gets blocked by the land's horizon.

76

ROCKING THE WAVES

What kind of man is this? Even the wind and the waves obey him!
—MARK 4:41

Waves are basically our planet's circulation system—they keep the oceans' water constantly on the move. Even though the oceans make up more than 70 percent of our planet's surface, the water in them doesn't stay in one spot. Some waves are tiny—so tiny you can barely see them. They're called *ripples*. Other waves, like *rogue waves*, can be more than 100 feet tall and can sink even the biggest ships! The top of a wave is called the *crest*, while the bottom is called a *trough*. Most waves are created by winds, but they can also be created by underwater currents, earthquakes, landslides under the water, or even underwater eruptions of volcanoes.

Jesus knows a thing or two about waves. After all, He made them. And, once, when He and His disciples were in a boat on the Sea of Galilee, a storm with huge waves hit. Jesus had fallen asleep, but when the waves started crashing over the boat, the terrified disciples hurried to wake Him up. Jesus got up and simply said, "Be still"—and the wind and the waves *stopped* (Mark 4:39). The disciples were amazed . . . and a little frightened. What kind of man could do that? The answer is . . . only Jesus. Because even though He was fully human, He was fully God at the same time. That means He had every bit of God's power and strength to command all things. So the next time you're in the middle of a terrifying storm—whether it's a storm of wind and waves or a storm of trouble—run to Jesus. He will see you safely through any kind of storm.

BE AMAZED

Tsunamis can be deadly. Caused by underwater earthquakes or volcanic eruptions, these waves start out small at only a few inches high. But as they get closer and closer to land, they can build up to more than 1,500 feet high!

Lord, sometimes this world can be pretty scary. Thank You for being a God I can always run to. I know You're always there for me. No matter how bad the storm is, I know You can calm it with just one word.

77

THE PALE BLUE DOT

[Christ] gave up his place with God and made himself nothing. . . . And when he was living as a man, he humbled himself and was fully obedient to God. He obeyed even when that caused his death—death on a cross.

—PHILIPPIANS 2:7–8

In 1977, NASA launched the Voyager 1 spacecraft into space with a mission to photograph our neighboring planets. Thirteen years later, after racing past Pluto, the farthest point in our solar system, at a speed of 40,000 miles per hour, Voyager 1 turned back toward Earth to snap a picture. That image became known as the "Pale Blue Dot." Taken from 4 billion miles away, the picture shook the scientific world. Why? Because it was the first time we got a glimpse of just how small our Earth really is in the expanse of the universe.

And that makes what Jesus did even more incredible! Jesus was equal with God, but He gave up His place in heaven and became one of us. He was born to Mary, a peasant woman, and her carpenter husband. His bed was a dusty manger in the town of Bethlehem. He grew up and lived and loved and healed and taught on this tiny "Pale Blue Dot." And then, obeying God, He willingly went to die on a cross, so every single person on this tiny blue dot could be forgiven when they call on Him.

Yes, we are indescribably small. Some like to say we don't really even matter. But when we look at Jesus, the One who gave up heaven to come down to this "Pale Blue Dot," we know the truth: we matter very much to God. He gave His own Son so we could know Him.

BE AMAZED

Scientists combined sixty different pictures together to make the one image called the "Pale Blue Dot." Each picture was made up of 640,000 pixels. Voyager 1 was so far away from the Earth that it took 5½ hours for each pixel to travel through space to Earth—not each picture, but each tiny pixel dot in the picture. It took *months* for the full images to make their way to us. Now that's a slow download!

Thank You, God, for sending Jesus to save me so I can know You. And help me remember that even though I am small, You can use me to do great things for You.

78

SINK YOUR TEETH INTO THIS

Now then, stand still and see this great thing the LORD is about to do before your eyes!
—1 SAMUEL 12:16 NIV

When you think about a shark, probably one of the first things you imagine is its teeth! More than 400 species of sharks are in the world, and they *all* have teeth! Lots and lots of them. That's because they also lose lots and lots of those teeth . . . as they rip and tear into their prey. *Yikes!* Sharks would

quickly starve without their teeth, so God gave them a unique teeth-replacement system.

Sharks' teeth are arranged in rows in their mouths, one behind the other. Some sharks have "only" 5 rows of teeth, but others, like the bull shark, have 50 rows! These rows basically act like conveyor belts. When one tooth is lost, another tooth from the row behind it pushes forward to take its place.

Sharks aren't the only creatures God takes care of in unique ways. He comes up with some pretty unusual ways to take care of His people too. Think about the Israelites who wandered and camped out in a desertlike wilderness for 40 years. Their shoes and clothes never wore out! Then there was Elijah—God fed him by sending ravens carrying bread and meat. And the widow of Zarephath? Even in the middle of a terrible famine, her jars of oil and flour never ran out. What a miracle! Many more examples of God's miraculous protection are in the Bible. The point of them all is that God takes care of His people, sometimes in amazing, creative, and miraculous ways. So you can always trust Him to take care of you. Just watch and see what creative ways He does it!

BE AMAZED

Sharks are born with a full set of teeth, unlike humans, who are born toothless! Sharks' teeth vary in shape, depending on the type of shark and what it eats. For example, the shortfin mako shark has razorlike teeth for tearing, while the zebra shark has flat teeth for crushing the shells of the mollusks it likes to eat.

Lord God, You are amazing in all the different ways You take care of Your creation. Open my eyes to see how You take care of me.

79

A MAGNETIC ATTRACTION

"Blessed are you when people insult you, persecute you and falsely say all kinds of evil against you because of me. Rejoice and be glad, because great is your reward in heaven."
—MATTHEW 5:11–12 NIV

Magnets are all around you. You might see some stuck on your refrigerator. How are magnets made, and what gives them their mysterious power of attraction? Remember that all matter—everything you can see and touch—is made up of millions of microscopic particles called *atoms*. Inside these atoms are even smaller particles called *electrons*. Usually, electrons zoom around every which way. But, sometimes, electrons all start zooming in the same direction, creating an invisible force called *magnetism*. This happens most often in metal objects made of iron or steel, creating a *magnet*. Magnetized objects attract other objects made of iron or steel.

Magnets have two *poles* (or ends)—a positive and a negative. If you put a positive end and a negative end near each other, they'll sort of jump together and stick. We call this *attraction*. But if you put two positive ends or two negative ends together, they'll push each other away (or *repel*). Go ahead and find some magnets, and try it for yourself—it's pretty cool to see.

This attracting and repelling is a lot like how people react to faith in Jesus sometimes. When you live your life loving and obeying God,

you shine like a light. That light will attract some people—and you'll have the wonderful opportunity to tell them about Jesus. But that light will repel others. They won't want to know about God. Some of them will just ignore you, but others may call you names and make fun of what you believe. Don't worry, though. Jesus said that when those things happen, you're actually blessed. Why? Because that means You're truly following Him.

Lord, help me live a "magnetic" life that pulls people to You. And when my faith repels some people, help me love them anyway.

BE AMAZED

Want to make your own magnet? It's easy. All you need are a couple of paper clips and a refrigerator magnet. Rub the magnet across one of the paper clips—but not back and forth—rub it across in the same direction, about 50 times, as fast as you can. Then, touch the magnetized paper clip to the other one—and watch it stick!

80

HARD AT HEART?

"I will give you a new heart and put a new spirit in you; I will remove from you your heart of stone and give you a heart of flesh."

—EZEKIEL 36:26 NIV

We tend to think of the Earth as being made of dirt, sand, and rocks, but that's just scratching the surface. The Earth is actually made up of five layers. The top layer is called the *crust*, and it's about 25 miles thick. (That's more than four Mount Everests stacked on top of each other.) Then there's the *upper mantle, lower mantle, outer core,* and *inner core*. It's the inner core that's at the center—the heart—of the Earth.

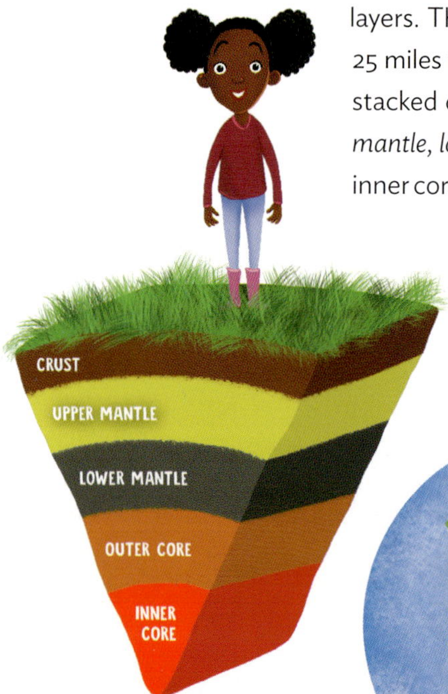

The inner core is pretty big at more than 750 miles across. And it's *really* hot. Scientists think its temperatures can be as high as 9,000 degrees Fahrenheit. *Whew!* Scientists also believe the core of the Earth is mostly made of iron. With temperatures in the thousands, you'd think that iron core would be melted, but

it's not. That's because extremely high pressures keep it squeezed into a hard, solid ball.

God made the Earth's core—its heart—to be hard. But that's not the way He made *your* core. *Your* heart was made to be soft. But it can get hard sometimes—like when someone hurts you, when you get angry or sad, or when too many things have gone wrong. How can your heart be made soft again, the way God created it to be? Start with prayer. Pour out your heart to God (Psalm 62:8). Tell Him everything. And then ask Him to clean your heart and wash all those hard feelings away (Psalm 51:10). He'll do it—He promised He would. Because God wants your heart to be soft . . . just like His.

God, caring about people can be hard. Sometimes it seems easier just not to care. When I start feeling that way, please wash those hard feelings away, and give me the courage and strength to care—especially when it's hard. Give me a soft heart, just like Yours.

BE AMAZED

The Mponeng gold mine in South Africa is the world's deepest mine. It stretches down more than 2.5 miles below the surface of the Earth. The temperatures at its bottom are so hot—up to 140 degrees Fahrenheit—that workers constantly pump an icy slush underground to make it safe.

81

ZAP TO IT

"Can you send lightning bolts on their way? Do the flashes of lightning report to you and say, 'Here we are'?"
—JOB 38:35

Have you ever watched lightning flash across the sky? It's beautiful and amazing and . . . so dangerous! Lightning is a gigantic burst of electricity that zaps across the sky with a brilliant flash of light and creates a booming crack called thunder. Lightning is caused by water and ice moving around inside a cloud, which creates an electric charge. When that charge gets strong enough, it bursts out as a bolt of lightning.

Did you know a spark of lightning can stretch out for miles? The longest distance a bolt has traveled is almost 200 miles! It also streaks through the air at a temperature of more than 50,000 degrees Fahrenheit! A single lightning strike can contain up to a billion volts of electricity. And every second, more than 100 lightning bolts strike somewhere on the Earth. That's an unbelievable amount of power!

God is so powerful that He *controls* the lightning. The Bible says, "God fills his hands with lightning" (Job 36:32), and His "voice makes the lightning flash" (Psalm 29:7). And the same God who commands lightning wants to pour His power into your life. How? Through prayer. It's that simple. Talking to God invites His power into your life. The Bible promises that when a child of God prays, He listens. Every single time. And that prayer "has great power and produces wonderful results" (James 5:16 NLT). So talk to God today with a prayer of your own. He's ready to listen—and to light up your life!

BE AMAZED

Lightning doesn't strike just in a thunderstorm. It can also strike during volcanic eruptions, forest fires, heavy snowstorms, and hurricanes.

Lord, Your power is too great for me to imagine—it is indescribable. And I pray that You will use that power in my life to make me into the person You created me to be.

82

WHAT'S THAT, YOU SAY?

Our love should not be only words and talk. Our love must be true love. And we should show that love by what we do.

—1 JOHN 3:18

People all over the world communicate using systems of words called *languages*. Which language do you speak? English is one of the most widely spoken languages in the world, with more than 1,500 million people able to speak it, though it's the native language for only about 375 million people. A

native language is the language you learn at home and grow up speaking. The Chinese language has the most native speakers at about 1 billion! Other popular languages are Hindi, Spanish, French, Arabic, Russian—the list could go on and on, to more than 7,000 different languages. Some are spoken by millions, some by a few thousand, and about 46 are spoken by only one person! (I wonder who they talk to!)

Some languages are pretty unusual. The Pirahã (pronounced pi-RAH-ha) language of Brazil has probably the simplest sound system with just 8 consonants and 3 vowels. The Taa language from Africa has more sounds than any other language, with just five kinds of clicks but 164 consonants and 44 vowels.

There are thousands of different ways to say what you want to say, but there's only one way to get your message across loud and clear—no matter what language you speak. That's by what you *do*. If you *say* you love Jesus, but you don't love and help others—your words mean nothing. On the other hand, if you try to be kind, helpful, and loving to everyone around you, your actions tell the world you really *do* love Jesus and want to be like Him.

BE AMAZED

One of the most beautiful languages in the world is found on La Gomera, a small island off the coast of Spain. This language—called silbo gomero—uses whistles instead of words! Because the island has so many mountains and ravines, yelling words doesn't work—they get all jumbled up. But a whistled message can be heard loud and clear!

Lord, I know my actions send a message to everyone around me. Please help me make that message a loving one that points people back to You.

83

ONLY ON EARTH

God stretches the northern sky out over empty space. And he hangs the earth on nothing.
—JOB 26:7

No other planet is quite like Earth—and definitely not in our solar system! In our solar system eight planets *orbit*, or circle around, the Sun. (Pluto lost its status as a "real" planet in 2006 and is now considered a "dwarf planet." *Bummer.*) Starting with those closest to the Sun, those eight planets are Mercury, Venus, Earth, Mars, Jupiter, Saturn, Uranus, and Neptune.

So why is Earth the only one with life? Well, let's take a look. Mercury is closest to the Sun, so it gets a little hot there—more than 800 degrees Fahrenheit! Venus is even hotter. Plus, its atmosphere is pure poison. Mars isn't hot, but it is cold and dry, with dust storms that can cover the whole planet! Ice is on Mars, but no liquid water to drink. Both Jupiter and Saturn are mostly made of hydrogen and helium gases, making it tough to stand up or breathe. The atmosphere of Uranus is full of methane gas—deadly, although it does have a pretty blue color. Neptune is 30 times farther away from the Sun than the Earth, which makes it very cold. It's also windy, with winds blowing up to 1,500 miles per hour! That's faster than the speed of sound—which, by the way, is 761 miles per hour.

Only Earth has just the right air, temperature, soil, and water conditions needed for life. It's almost as if Earth was designed for life. Oh wait, it was! Genesis tells us that God created the Earth and gave it everything needed for life—the Sun and Moon, water and skies. Then He filled it with life—plants and animals and people. And God said the Earth and everything in it "was very good" (Genesis 1:31).

Thank You, God, for the Earth you've given me to live on. And thank You for Jesus, who gives me heaven to live in forever.

BE AMAZED

Scientists kicked Pluto out of the planet club back in 2006, but now they think a ninth planet might exist somewhere past Neptune. They call it "Planet Nine," and scientists think it's about 10 times the mass of the Earth and 5,000 times the mass of the dwarf planet Pluto. No one's seen the mystery planet yet, but scientists are still looking!

84

BLOOM WHERE YOU'RE PLANTED

I have learned the secret of being happy at any time in everything that happens. . . . I can do all things through Christ because he gives me strength.
—PHILIPPIANS 4:12–13

Plants need just a few things to grow: sunlight, water, air, and nutrients. Some plants—like trees and grass—get what they need in a pretty simple way. Dirt gives them their nutrients, rain gives them their water, and plants find sunlight and air all around them. But God made other plants to be a little more creative to get what they need.

For example, some desert plants have very long roots, allowing them to "dig" deep for underground water. Many desert plants, like cacti, are able to store water from rare desert rainfalls. In the rainforest, where it rains more than 100 inches every year, plants have "drip tips" that quickly send all that extra water dripping away so their leaves don't get moldy. Arctic plants grow low to the ground and close together to survive the bitter cold.

God also created *you* to bloom where you're planted—no matter where you are and no matter what's happening around you. How? By depending on Jesus and being thankful for all He's given you. If you're having the absolute best day ever, it's easy to bloom with happiness and thankfulness. When you're having the worst day ever, it's a bit tougher. But you can always be thankful for Jesus! Put your roots in His love, let God's Word feed you, and reach out to the world around you. Before you know it, you'll be blooming right where you're planted.

Dear God, no matter what's happening in my day today, I know I have many things to be thankful for. Open my eyes to see them, and help me bloom wherever You plant me.

BE AMAZED

Fire is the enemy of all plants, right? Wrong! Not the jack pine tree (also known by its scientific name of *Pinus banksiana*). This tree's seeds are stuck in resin-filled cones, which are basically glued shut. (Think of resin as being like superglue!) Since the resin is so strong, cones can stay sealed shut for years . . . until a forest fire sweeps through, melts the resin, and allows the cones to open and spill out the seeds. That's part of God's miraculous design to replant the forest after a fire.

85

WHAT A TANGLED WEB WE WEAVE

The Lord detests lying lips, but he delights in those who tell the truth.
—PROVERBS 12:22 NLT

Spiders . . . they're the stuff of nightmares and horror movies. But they're also quite amazing—in an icky sort of way. Spiders are hunters. Most spiders eat insects, but fishing spiders fish for . . . well . . . fish. Huntsman spiders, which can have a horrifying 12-inch leg span, trap frogs and lizards. And some of the world's biggest spiders catch birds and bats in their massive webs!

All spiders make silk, but not all spiders use it to spin webs. Silk also protects spiders' eggs, helps spiders move, and provides shelter. Web-spinning spiders use silk to create elaborate traps to catch their dinner. Because the webs are nearly invisible, insects fly into the webs and get trapped in the sticky threads. When an insect gets trapped in a web, a spider feels the vibration of the insect's struggles and hurries to wrap the bug in more silk. Because it can't eat solid food, the spider injects its prey with digestive juices, turning the prey into a liquid mush for the spider to suck up. Sort of a spider's version of a milkshake. *Yuck!*

A spider's web is a sticky and deadly trap—and it is a lot like the trap of lying. The first lie you spin may be small, almost invisible, so you think no one will even see it. But someone usually does. So you spin a bigger lie to cover up the first one—and then an even bigger lie to cover up *that* one. Soon you're surrounded by a whole web of lies, and the one who ends up getting trapped and tangled is *you*. So don't ever spin that first lie. Tell the truth, and keep yourself out of sticky situations.

God, sometimes it seems easier to tell a lie—like when I don't want to get into trouble. Please give me the courage and the strength to always tell the truth.

Wolf Spider

BE AMAZED

Not all spiders catch their meals by spinning webs. The wolf spider stalks its prey and catches it. Jumping spiders move fast and have very good eyesight. Can you guess how they catch their prey? That's right—they jump on it!

86

TAP INTO THE POWER

God's power is very great for us who believe. That power is the same as the great strength God used to raise Christ from death.

—EPHESIANS 1:19–20

Electricity . . . it powers our lights, our heating and cooling, our computers, our games, our phones, and so much more. Life would be very different without electricity.

We get our electricity from many different sources that can be sorted into two groups: renewable resources and nonrenewable resources. *Renewable resources* are those that can be used over and over again, and they won't run out. These include solar energy from the Sun, wind power, and water (or hydro) power. It also includes geothermal power, which uses the heat from below the Earth's surface, and biomass power, which burns plant and animal waste (like cow poop!) to create heat and steam—which is then turned into electricity. *Nonrenewable resources* cannot be reused and may run out someday. Coal, oil, and natural gas are examples of nonrenewable resources.

Whatever the source of electricity, its power keeps all the world's machines going. But there's a different kind of power that keeps Christians going—and it's 100 percent renewable. It's the power of God. When you're tired or when you're not sure what to do, that's the time to tap into the power of God. He knows everything (Psalm 147:5), He promises to answer when you call to Him (Psalm 120:1), and there's nothing that's impossible for Him (Matthew 19:26). No matter what you're facing, God has the power to carry you through it. So say a prayer, right this very second, and tap into the power of God.

Lord, Your power is so great that I can't even imagine it. You created the stars, the planets, and me! And the really amazing thing is that You promise to use Your power in my life. Thank You, God!

BE AMAZED

Benjamin Franklin wasn't the first person to discover electricity, but he is famous for his lightning experiment. According to legend, he flew a kite that had a metal key attached into a thundercloud, and he was able to get electricity from the lightning in the cloud. We don't know if the details of that legendary experiment are true, but we do know Franklin invented the lightning rod—a metal pole that safely carries the electrical power of lightning away from buildings during a thunderstorm.

87

WAIT FOR IT

Wait patiently for the LORD. Be brave and courageous. Yes, wait patiently for the LORD.
—PSALM 27:14 NLT

The hummingbird is a flying powerhouse. It can reach speeds of up to 30 miles per hour, and up to 60 miles per hour when it dives—that's almost as fast as your car drives on the highway! Its wings beat up to 80 flaps per second, depending on which direction it's flying. To power those wings, a hummingbird takes about 250 breaths per minute, and its heart beats 1,200 times per minute.

For comparison, your heart beats only between 70 and 100 times per minute!

All that power is packed into tiny hummingbird packages. The calliope hummingbird is just 3 inches long, making it the smallest bird in North America. But the bee hummingbird of Cuba is even tinier. At only 2.25 inches long, it's the smallest bird in the world. The ruby-throated hummingbird weighs about 3 grams—lighter than an American nickel, which weighs 4.5 grams. But the most amazing thing about hummingbirds is the way they can fly! They dart in and out between flowers—flying upright, upside down, sideways, and backward. They can even "slam on the brakes" and hover in midair.

BE AMAZED

The hummingbird lays one of the smallest eggs of any bird in the world. How small? The ruby-throated hummingbird lays an egg about the size of a pea. The mama bird then tucks those tiny eggs into a walnut-sized nest made from spiderwebs and bits of plants.

Sometimes God will ask you to stop and hover—not in midair, but in your prayers. You see, God *always* answers your prayers. Sometimes He says yes right away, and sometimes He says no right away. But other times, God asks you to wait—to "hover"—for an answer. He wants you to be still and not try to control things to get the answer you want. God wants you to trust Him and wait while He works everything in your life in just the right way. So what can you do while you wait? "Hover" close to God! Keep praying (Luke 18:1–8). And keep trusting that God started answering your prayer request before you even asked it (Isaiah 65:24)!

Lord, You know I'm not very good at waiting. So please help me to be patient while You work on Your perfect answer for me.

88

MUSCLE UP

Those who know the Lord trust him. He will not leave those who come to him.
—PSALM 9:10

Muscles are what keep you moving—walking, jumping, running, skipping, leapfrogging . . . well . . . you get the idea. They're also what keep you sitting still, helping hold your back straight and your head up high. Some muscles are easy to see, like the ones in your arms and legs. But there are lots of other muscles you probably don't even realize you're using—like the muscles in your heart, lungs, stomach, eyes, and ears. (Muscles inside your ears? Who knew?) Without muscles, your body simply couldn't live.

Some muscles, like those in the heart and digestive system, work all the time and get plenty of exercise all on their own. But other muscles, like those in the arms and legs, need to be exercised every day. All your muscles need the energy that comes from eating the right kinds of foods—not too much junk! And even those muscles that never stop working need the healing that comes from rest. These three things—exercise, food, and rest—keep your physical muscles in top shape.

But what about your spiritual muscles? The muscles of your faith—what keeps them strong? The same things, really: exercise, food, and rest. You exercise your faith by getting up each morning and choosing to trust that God loves you and will take care of you, no matter what happens. You feed your faith by reading God's Word every

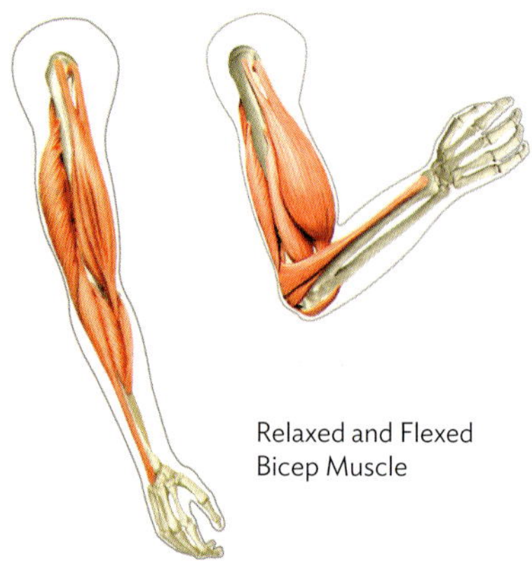

Relaxed and Flexed Bicep Muscle

single day. And you heal from the hard times of this world by resting during your quiet time spent talking to and listening to God. So get up and get some exercise—for your muscles and your faith.

Lord, teach me to take care of this body that You created. And help me remember that my faith needs to be taken care of too.

BE AMAZED

The hardest-working muscle in your body is the heart—it never takes a break, and it keeps pumping twenty-four hours a day, seven days a week. The smallest muscle is the *stapedius*, which is inside your middle ear. It's less than 2 millimeters long. And the biggest muscles? Those would be a group of muscles called the *gluteus maximus*. (Here's a hint: they're the ones you sit on!)

89

WHAT GOD SEES

Nothing in all creation is hidden from God's sight.
—HEBREWS 4:13 NIV

Did you know that on a clear night, away from the city lights and using only your eyes, you can see all the way to the Andromeda Galaxy, which is located an astonishing 2.5 million light-years from Earth? And on a really good night, you can see all the way to a star called Deneb, one of the brightest stars in our Milky Way Galaxy. Scientists aren't sure exactly how far away Deneb is, but they think it's at least 9 *quadrillion* miles away—or 9,000,000,000,000,000. That's a lot of zeroes! God made your eyes amazingly powerful so you can see just a bit of His magnificent creation.

But as powerful as your eyes are, God's eyes are even more powerful. He can see the farthest star in the farthest galaxy of the universe. He can also see the shortest hair on the left leg of the tiniest bug. *And* He can see every hair on your head—and count every single one (Luke 12:7). God sees absolutely everything!

And He sees you—perfectly and completely. But when God looks at you, He doesn't look at just the outside—your clothes, your hair, or your nose. God looks much deeper than that. He looks at your heart, and He sees all the things that are filling it. He sees the worries and the doubts, what makes you happy and what scares you. He also sees the anger, the jealousy, and all those secret sins you think no one else knows. God already knows everything in your heart, so you can tell Him anything at all. When you talk to Him, He promises to fill your heart with peace. Ask God to help your heart look more like His—filled with wonderful things like love, joy, and kindness.

God, thank You for giving me eyes to see the wonder and beauty of Your creation all around me. Help me see how I can be more like You today.

BE AMAZED

Your eyes blink about 12 times every minute—that's more than 10,000 blinks every day (not counting when you're asleep, of course). Each blink lasts about 0.3 seconds, which means you have your eyes closed for more than 50 minutes every day!

90

A MIND TO SEE

Do not be shaped by this world. Instead be changed within by a new way of thinking. Then you will be able to decide what God wants for you. And you will be able to know what is good and pleasing to God and what is perfect.

—ROMANS 12:2

Starfish can do some amazing things, like regrow a limb if one is broken off. But one of the weirdest things about starfish is how they eat. First, a hungry starfish will wrap its arms around a mussel or clam and pull the shell open just enough to . . . *push its own stomach out through its mouth and into the shell.* After digesting the animal, the starfish then slides its stomach back into its own body. That sounds like something out of an alien movie!

Another unusual thing about the starfish is that it has an eye at the end of each arm. But the starfish doesn't have an actual brain to tell it what it's seeing. Instead, nerves run from its mouth to each of its eyes, and sensors in its many tubelike "feet" actually find food. So the starfish is perfectly able to move and eat and do all that it needs to live, but it can't think. The starfish can't "see" what path it should take—it just goes where its body tells it to go.

That's where you're different. Not only do you have eyes to see, but you also have a mind to think. And God wants you to use your mind. He's laid out a path for your life—a path that will lead you all the way to heaven. It's a path made of wise choices, the words of the Bible, and loving others. It's a path that God knows perfectly and promises to lead you on.

Lord, teach me something new about You every day. Open my eyes, my mind, and my heart to see You in this world all around me. Lead me on Your path of life, and open my mind to where You're leading me.

BE AMAZED

More than 2,000 different types of starfish are in the world. Most of them have only 5 arms, but others have as many as 40 arms. The sunflower starfish is one of the largest kinds of starfish. It has 24 arms and can grow as big as 40 inches from arm tip to arm tip!

91

RAIN, RAIN . . . DON'T GO AWAY

"Your Father causes the sun to rise on good people and on bad people. Your Father sends rain to those who do good and to those who do wrong."
—MATTHEW 5:45

You probably think of rain as water droplets falling from the sky. But rain's technical name is *precipitation*, and it includes hail, sleet, and snow. Rain begins way up in the clouds as ice or snow crystals, and a single droplet can "float" up there for 10 days. When the raindrop does finally fall, it can plummet to the Earth at speeds of up to 22 miles per hour! For comparison, a snowflake floats gracefully through the sky at just 2 to 4 miles per hour—taking almost an hour to reach the ground. Some places on the Earth get very little rain, while other places get a lot. But every single spot on Earth gets *some* rain.

That's kind of like troubles. Everybody has them, both good people and bad people. It can be hard to understand why bad things sometimes happen to good people who love God and try to do what's right. And it can be just as hard to understand why good things—like fame, success, and riches—sometimes happen to bad people. But don't let this worry or upset you. God allows the Sun to shine and the rain to fall on both good *and* bad people. It's all part of His plan, and His plan is perfect. In the end, God will use all things—blessings and troubles—to bring about good for His people, and they display His glory to the whole Earth (Romans 8:28).

Dear God, there are so many things I don't understand, but there's one thing I do know: You are always good, and I can always trust You. Thank You for having good plans for my life!

BE AMAZED

You might think the least rainy place on Earth would be a desert, but it's not. It's Antarctica, which gets only about 6.5 inches of rain or snow each year. On the other hand, the rainiest place in the world is Lloro, Colombia, in South America. It gets more than 530 inches of rain a year!

92

WANNA PLAY?

Ask the animals, and they will teach you. Or ask the birds of the air, and they will tell you. . . . Every one of these knows that the hand of the Lord has done this.

—JOB 12:7–9

Have you ever watched a kitten bat at a piece of string? Or sent a puppy running to fetch a ball? Or watched a group of otters at the zoo twisting and whirling through the water? Just like you, animals like to play. Baby horses chase each other and toss around sticks and rags. Baby kangaroos love to play-fight with their moms, and certain kinds of fish will jump playfully over turtles and twigs.

But it's dolphins that are perhaps best known for their playfulness. Of course, they can put on quite a show at aquariums, but even in the wild, dolphins can be seen leaping high into the air. Spinner dolphins launch themselves high in the air and spin around and around, while dusky dolphins like to add in a flip.

Scientists believe animals play for several different reasons: to practice life skills, to communicate with each other, or perhaps for the sheer joy of playing in God's creation! That last reason may be the very best reason for all of us to play.

God created this world for His people not only to live in and take care of, but also to *enjoy*. God didn't have to make the flowers in so many different, beautiful colors. He didn't have to create puddles to jump in, trees to climb, or hills to go rolling down—but He did. He didn't have to make so many kinds of delicious fruits (and vegetables!), but He did. Take time to enjoy all the wonders of this world that God made. Let the animals teach *you* a thing or two—go outside and play!

BE AMAZED

Everyone knows puppies and kittens play . . . but *crocodiles*? It's true! Scientists have observed crocodiles using their snouts to blow bubbles in the water and snap playfully at waves. They've also been spotted playing with flowers and carrying them in their teeth. These scary, scaly beasts have even been known to give each other piggyback rides!

Lord, thank You for all the wonders of this world You've made. Open my eyes to see them all, and open my heart to enjoy them. Your creation is marvelous!

93

THE HEART OF THE MATTER

The Lord looks down from heaven. He sees every person. . . . He made their hearts. He understands everything they do.
—PSALM 33:13, 15

When you put your hand on your chest, do you know what that thump-thumping is you feel? It's your heart. Do you know when it started thumping? After being in your mom's womb for only 22 days! Now that you're much bigger, your heart has a lot more work to do. It's grown to about the size of your fist, and it now pumps blood through the 60,000 miles of blood vessels in your body!

Your heart is amazing because the One who hung the stars is the same One who shaped and formed your heart. But when you think about the word *heart*, you probably think of more than just a body part thump-thumping along, don't you? You think about all the emotions and feelings it holds—like happiness, sadness, excitement, and fear. And while the physical heart inside your body isn't really where all those emotions live, the heart is where people say they feel them. The incredible fact is that the God who's big enough to know all the secrets of the universe also loves you so much that He knows all the emotions of your heart and exactly when you feel them.

God knows when you're frightened, worried, happy, or sad—and every emotion in between. *And He understands you*. No matter how hard life gets or how dark this world seems, God has a plan to help you, and He knows just the right way to comfort you. Check out this awesome promise: "I am the Lord your

God. I am holding your right hand. And I tell you, 'Don't be afraid. I will help you'" (Isaiah 41:13). God's always with you—with every beat of your heart.

God, thank You for this heart You've given me. Please fill it with Your love, Your courage, and Your strength. And help me always to hide Your Word inside my heart.

BE AMAZED

How fast does your heart beat? For the average person, the heart beats about 60–100 times each minute. If you multiply that by all the minutes in a day, your heart beats more than *100,000 times* a day. And it can beat even faster—when you're exercising, excited, nervous, or scared.

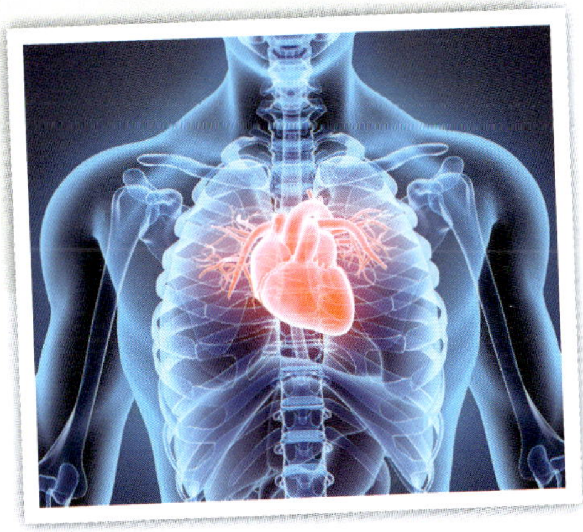

94

WHICH WAY DOES THE WIND BLOW?

Stand strong. Do not let anything move you. Always give yourselves fully to the work of the Lord. You know that your work in the Lord is never wasted.
—1 CORINTHIANS 15:58

Wind can be mysterious, even alarming! You can't see it, but you know it's there when it brushes across your face or makes the leaves shake. And you

can hear it coming as it howls through the trees. But what is wind? And what makes it blow? Wind is simply moving air. That movement is caused by differences in the air pressure—which are caused by differences in temperature. Warm air has a lower pressure and wants to rise. As it rises, cooler air (with its higher pressure) moves in and takes its place. This movement of warmer and cooler air is what creates wind.

Winds like the *trade winds* near the equator and the *polar winds* at the North and South Poles almost always blow the same way. But local winds can change directions several times a day, depending on what's happening in the weather around them.

People can be like the wind sometimes. They change their direction—what they say and how they act—depending on what's happening around them or who's standing nearby. Do you do that? Do you say whatever other people want to hear? Or change the way you act—even doing something you know is wrong—just to fit in? Don't do that! God doesn't want you to change direction like the wind. Instead, "stand strong" for what you believe, stand up for what's right, and stand up for God. People may laugh or make fun or even worse. But remember that when God is on your side, no one can stand against you (Romans 8:31).

BE AMAZED

Cape Blanco in Oregon is one of the windiest places on the Earth. Strong winter storms often create winds that roar through at more than 100 miles per hour. But the honor of the windiest spot in the world belongs to Port Martin, an abandoned research base in Antarctica. Winds there blow at an average of 40 miles per hour throughout the year!

Lord, when everyone around me seems to be changing like the wind, help me stand strong and stand up for You. I praise You because You never change!

95

WHAT SCIENTISTS DON'T KNOW

"Just as the heavens are higher than the earth, so are my ways higher than your ways. And my thoughts are higher than your thoughts."
—ISAIAH 55:9

Scientists have discovered a lot of amazing things, like how fast the Earth spins and how far the Earth is from the Sun. Scientists know how to build rocket ships that blast into space as well as submarines that travel through the seas.

But there are countless things scientists *don't* know. Things like how many stars are in the Milky Way or how many galaxies are in the universe. They don't know what's inside a black hole or what lives at the very bottom of the deepest ocean. Scientists don't know exactly how a baby forms in his mother's womb. That means they aren't entirely sure how you and I became . . . you and I.

Why are there so many things scientists don't know yet? Because God created this universe—and everything in it. And He's more creative than anyone could ever dream of being. What's truly amazing is that

God gave us the ability to learn about and explore His magnificent creation. What scientists do know, as well as the things they don't yet know, gives us all the more reason to marvel at God's *indescribable* creativity and power. But even though God is indescribable, there are countless things we can know about Him.

For example, you can know He loves you, and His love will never change (Jeremiah 31:3). You can know He'll save you from your sins if you'll believe in Jesus and follow Him (John 3:16). You can know He has a perfect and wonderful plan for your life, even if you don't always understand it (Jeremiah 29:11).

BE AMAZED

In the Bible, a man named Job lost everything, and he asked God, "Why?" God answered him with a whole list of things men and women will never understand—things like where the sea begins (Job 38:16) and where light and darkness live (Job 38:19). Read Job 38. How many other things about God's creation are just too wonderful for us to know?

Dear God, there are so many, many things about this world I'll never understand. But I do understand You love me and only want the best for me. I will trust You always. And I'm so thankful I will never stop learning about You!

The Milky Way Galaxy

96

THE SUPREME SURVIVOR

"Don't worry, because I am with you. Don't be afraid, because I am your God. I will make you strong and will help you. I will support you with my right hand that saves you."
—ISAIAH 41:10

The tardigrade, or water bear, isn't a bear at all. Rather, it's a tiny little invertebrate that lives in moss, on plants, in sand, in freshwater, and in the sea. Tardigrades are among the few animals that can be found both on the highest mountains and in the deepest seas. These tiny creatures are only about

1.5 millimeters long (just slightly more than the thickness of a dime), but the tardigrade is fierce. Its mouth is full of daggerlike teeth, which it uses to tear into algae and other tiny animals.

These tough little creatures can live in boiling water and in the deepest trenches of the oceans. They can survive for more than 10 years without a drop of water. Scientists in Japan even froze a couple of tardigrades for 30 years—and when thawed out, they were still alive! God gave this little creature—that you've probably never heard of—everything it needs to survive.

BE AMAZED

To test just how tough the tardigrade is, scientists launched some into space in 2007. Since no spacesuits were small enough for the tardigrades, they were exposed to the conditions of open space for 10 days. In spite of cosmic rays and the lack of air in the vacuum of space, most of the tardigrades survived!

And how much more will God do for you, His most prized creation? In this world, you'll face troubles, temptations, and fears so fierce that you might think you can't survive. But you can because God is on your side. There's no trouble He can't handle (Matthew 19:26). There's no temptation He can't help you defeat (1 Corinthians 10:13). And there's no need to worry or fear (Matthew 6:25–34) because He will give you everything you need not only to survive, but to thrive, as His treasured child. God created *you* to be an extreme survivor, and He's with you no matter what the conditions!

Dear God, there are so many tough things that I have to face in this world. Thank You for giving me everything I need to get through them. You are stronger than the toughest obstacle I'll ever face!

97

POLLUTION SOLUTION

Do everything without complaining or arguing.
—PHILIPPIANS 2:14

Pollution happens when something gets dumped into the environment that doesn't belong. Different kinds of pollution are in the world, but the three main kinds are *air, water,* and *land pollution*.

Air pollution can be a big problem because all living things need air. This kind of pollution happens when fossil fuels—like coal, oil, and gas—are burned. Car fumes and factory smoke are examples of air pollution. Water becomes polluted when chemicals, detergents, garbage, or even sewage gets dumped into streams, rivers, or oceans. Land is mostly polluted by trash—from litter

on the side of the road to massive garbage dumps and landfills.

All that pollution is bad for the environment and bad for you. But there are ways you can help: Walk or ride your bike instead of taking a car. Pick up litter and put it in the trash. Recycle as much as you can. Turn off lights and electronics when you aren't using them. These may not seem like big things, but even small actions can add up to a lot!

One other kind of pollution you can help get rid of is *attitude pollution*. This happens when you dump whining or angry words into the environment around you. Like all pollution, this hurts the environment around you, and that means it also hurts you. Times will come when you're angry or upset because you have to do something you don't want to do. But throwing a fit or grumbling won't change a thing. Instead, take a deep breath and smile. Then tackle that chore as if you're doing it for God (Colossians 3:23)—because whatever you do for others, you also do for God. Complaining pollutes the air around you, but a joyful spirit makes the environment better for everyone!

BE AMAZED

One of the strangest pollution stories happened when a ship somehow spilled its cargo into middle of the Pacific Ocean. What was the cargo? Twenty-eight thousand rubber duckies—along with a few rubber turtles, beavers, and frogs. Some of those duckies floated thousands of miles, all the way to Alaska!

God, some things I just really don't want to do—like cleaning my room and taking out the trash. But help me remember that when I serve others, I also serve You. Help me make the environment around me better and brighter with a joyful spirit!

98

WATER, WATER EVERYWHERE

"Your Father knows what you need before you ask him."
—MATTHEW 6:8 NIV

Water—we use it every single day. We drink it, cook with it, and wash with it. (Every day, right?) It helps our food and flowers grow. We use it to fight fires and produce electricity. We even play in it with sports like swimming, ice skating, and snow skiing. Water covers more than 70 percent of the Earth and makes up about 60 percent of our bodies.

Water itself is made up of two different elements: hydrogen and oxygen. Two atoms of hydrogen join with a single atom of oxygen to make H_2O—or, as we like to call it—water. The word *water* is usually used to describe the liquid form of this combination, while *ice* is the solid form, and *steam* or *vapor* is the gas form.

Water is a must-have for life. You can survive about three weeks without eating, but you can only go about three days without water. Water makes up your saliva so you can swallow. It flushes the waste and poisons out of your body. It cushions your brain, moistens your eyes, lubricates your joints, keeps your body temperature balanced, and helps deliver oxygen to all of your body. Not only do *you* need it, but so does every single plant and animal on the Earth. Water is pretty important stuff.

BE AMAZED

Water (or H_2O) can be a solid, liquid, or gas—depending on its temperature. It freezes into a solid at 32 degrees Fahrenheit and boils into a gas at 212 degrees Fahrenheit. But under just the right amount of pressure and at just the right temperature, water can be all three! This is called the *triple point*.

Maybe that's why God made it on the second day of creation (Genesis 1:6–8), *before* He made any plants, animals, or people. God knew everything would need water, so He provided water *before* it was even needed. That's just what God does. He knows everything you need—before you ask for it or even know you need it. And He's already got a plan to get you what you need.

God, thank You for the gift of water and for all it does for me. Thank You most of all for watching over me and making sure I have everything I truly need.

99

FRUIT-FULL

The Holy Spirit produces this kind of fruit in our lives: love, joy, peace, patience, kindness, goodness, faithfulness, gentleness, and self-control.
—GALATIANS 5:22–23 NLT

In the world are two kinds of living things: producers and consumers. *Producers* are things like plants and trees. They use a process called *photosynthesis* to turn sunlight, water, and carbon dioxide into a kind of sugar, which is then used to fuel plants as they grow. Plants basically *produce* their own food, and this fuel gives them energy to grow into fruits, veggies, leaves, stems, and flowers.

Animals, on the other hand, are *consumers*. That's because they can't make their own food. Instead, they *consume* food, which their bodies use as fuel for energy. Three different kinds of consumers are in the world. The first are *herbivores*, and they eat only plants. The second are *carnivores*, and they eat only meat. And the third are *omnivores* because they eat both animals and plants. If you eat a hamburger and fries, *you* are an omnivore!

Since you eat to survive, you are a consumer. But God also wants you to be a producer—of spiritual fruit. No, He doesn't mean apples and oranges. God wants you to produce the fruit of the Spirit, which includes love, joy, peace, patience, kindness, goodness, faithfulness, gentleness, and self-control. You can't produce this fruit on your own, but that's okay—God's given you His Spirit to help you. Just as plants can't produce fruit without sunlight, water, and air, you can't produce the fruit of the Spirit without exposure to God's Word, His voice in prayer, and the light of His love. When you decide to follow God, He sends His Spirit to live inside you. The Spirit will help you talk to God, understand His Word, *and* produce fruit. He'll make you truly fruit-full!

Dear God, please fill me with the light of Your Word and with Your Spirit. Nourish me so I can produce Your kind of fruit!

BE AMAZED

People often say you should eat plenty of fruits and vegetables, but figuring out which are which might be tougher than you think. Plums, peaches, and pears are actually part of the rose family. And pumpkins, zucchini, and peas aren't veggies at all—they're fruits!

100

HERE'S YOUR CHANGE

We are being changed to be like [the Lord]. This change in us brings more and more glory. And it comes from the Lord, who is the Spirit.
—2 CORINTHIANS 3:18

***Metamorphosis*—it's what happens when an animal changes its body from one form to another.** Butterflies and frogs are probably the best-known examples of animals that go through metamorphosis. The butterfly begins life as an egg that hatches into a caterpillar. After growing and shedding its skin several times, the caterpillar turns into a chrysalis, and the outer layer of the chrysalis hardens to become a protective shell. Within the chrysalis, the caterpillar completely transforms into a beautiful butterfly.

The frog also starts life as an egg. The egg grows into a tadpole that lives in the water. Over the next few weeks, the tadpole's mouth gets wider, its eyes bulge out, and its tail shrinks and shrinks, until it completely disappears. Just a few more changes and it transforms into a frog—ready to hop away to its first jumping contest!

If you were to look at the before-and-after pictures of butterflies and caterpillars (or tadpoles and frogs), you'd think they were completely different creatures. But that's what metamorphosis is—a complete change.

A Bullfrog Tadpole

If *you* could go through a metamorphosis, what would you change? Would you want wings